MW00585870

Crashing An American Wake

An Irishman's tale of loss, struggle, war, **the American dream**
and a promise fulfilled

By Colleen Ann Keane

The Keane Brothers in Dublin around 1928

Edited by: Cindy Yurth

mrsswanee@me.com

Photos by: Colleen Keane, Tarmon National School, historic family photos and photos preserved at the Castlerea library, County Roscommon, Ireland

Starred photos originally published in the Navajo Times

Copyright – © Colleen Keane, 2021

For more information or for use of any photos or passages email colleenannkeane@ gmail.com. Or write Colleen Keane, P.O. Box 40256, Albuquerque, NM 87196, USA

Paperback ISBN: 978-1-66780-784-3

This book is dedicated to:

My beautiful and brilliant daughter Joanna and the beautiful and brilliant students at the Tarmon National school in Castlerea, Ireland, County Roscommon who strive to be conscious and responsible human beings looking to the past for lessons, the present for actualization and the future for hope.

My brother Brian, my cousin Noel, Rita Morgan, Elizabeth Kenny, Jean Higgins, Finbar McNamara, Anthony Tuohy and Michael Hanley for their support, encouragement and historical memories.

Jacinta Greene Beatty of Castlerea who supported the publication of this book from the first day I met her standing in line at the Bank of Ireland.

Martin Dunn and Jimmy Ganly of the County Roscommon Historical Society.

Ellen and Leo Finnegan and Jean Higgins of the Williamstown Heritage Society of County Galway.

Veterans of all wars who suffered and who are still suffering from post-traumatic stress disorder.

My adventurous, courageous and loving father.

TABLE OF CONTENTS

Introduction

My dad seldom talked about his life in Ireland before immigrating to America.

Growing up, the only references to Irish culture and history my brothers Brian and Jerry and I had were of my dad's favorite dish, corned beef and cabbage, and celebrating St. Patrick's Day.

On St. Patrick's Day, we'd have big parties in our basement, which my mom turned into a bar complete with blackened walls, a keg, a lineup of whiskeys and liquors, neon-hopping beer and whisky signs and piped-in music from upstairs. It's during those celebrations my dad gave us a glimpse of the 'old country', referring to the land of his birth as a long-gone lifetime away. Holding up a shot of whiskey, he'd sing with Irish friends, "Danny Boy" and "When Irish Eyes are Smiling."

By the time I was in grade school he had lost his brogue. But, on celebrations like this a gentle lilt surfaced ever so subtly. After the songs, spirits and many toasts to his native home and family, the view into our Irish history and culture faded away. My brothers and I never knew our grandparents, aunts (except Aunt Mary who emigrated years before him), uncles, cousins or the Irish culture and history that ran in our blood.

As time went on, I realized how much we lost, cut off from our Irish heritage.

Crashing an American Wake fills in the blanks as I learned about my Irish history and the extraordinary role my dad played in Ireland and America. As a young child he witnessed the rising of the Irish rebellion; as a teenager, the War of Independence and the Civil War. As a young adult he immigrated to America, weathered the Great Depression by joining President Franklin D. Roosevelt's Civilian Conservation Corps and as an American citizen, husband and father, enlisted in World War II to fight against Hitler's worldwide tyranny.

During WWII, he fought next to members of Native American tribes, who like himself understood first-hand the loss of human rights under cruel colonial governments and the fight for independence.

As a reporter for the Navajo Times for many years, I bring attention to commonalities between the occupation of the U.S. on Native American lands and the British occupation of Ireland. There are many. Colonial cruelty has no borders. I also bring attention to the resistance efforts on both sides of the Atlantic as Ireland and Native Nations decolonize.

As a journalist, I approach this more personal story creatively. It's both factual and imagined (*in italics*) about my family's Irish history and how my father crashed his American Wake to let his family back home know just how things turned out.

Chapter 1 –
The promise

My dad's American Wake was in 1930, 91 years ago.

He was 22 when his mom, my grandmother, Bridget Connor Keane, opened up her cottage in Bookalagh, a townland (about 160 acres) known for its boggy fields in the midlands of Ireland, to give him his sending off the night before he left for America, most likely never to be seen again.

The day before his American Wake, he went from house to house, as was the custom, to tell of his leaving and invite everyone he spoke to and their kin to his living memorial, a time both joyous and somber. For sure there would be an abundance of food and drink. And soon as the music started playing, the dancing and storytelling would carry through the evening into the morning. Neighbors came, including those in Ballymoe, a nearby village.

Born in 1908, he was known as Brian Keane. His birth name was Bernard after his father. His birth record shows he was born June 20th, but I always thought he was born on May 30th because that's when we celebrated his birthday. He never mentioned any discrepancy about the day of his birth.

In the States, he was known as Barney. He was a man of few words and a quick wit. He kept his past to himself; some say that's just how it used to be in those days.

In 1986, he had his final sending-off. He was 78.

Like his first wake, friends came from all around — Detroit, where he first settled, and across Toledo, Ohio where my brothers and I grew up.

The two wakes lean like bookends to a life of a man I simply knew as Dad, but who was much more – he was a reflection of the 20th Century.

The photos

Sometime after my dad died, my mom gave me his Irish passport and old photographs. It was the first time I'd seen him as a young man.

"That's your dad there," she said pointing to the young man standing in the middle. On either side of him, his brother James on his left and his brother John on the right, according to a couple of sources. I imagine my dad carried the photo with him as he crossed the Atlantic, tucked in with his passport, where I now keep it. The photo, which was made into a postcard, had no writing on the address side. All those years, it was the only memento my father kept, along with his Irish passport, serving as a memory of the day the brothers traveled to Dublin and had their photo taken at the Franco and Sackville studio on O'Connell Street.

In the photo that's the cover of this book, there's not a smile between them as they glare straight into the camera wearing their Sunday best, dark three-piece woolen suits, buttoned up white shirts, waistcoats and wide ties.

Like their outfits, their hair is in the style of the day, abundant on the top and close-shaved on the side.

My dad's eyes seem to express a sorrow that has beset him, for maybe he realizes more than ever how much he's going to miss his brothers, his mom, his neighbors and friends. He's 20 years old and the writing is on the wall for him to immigrate to America.

It's a difficult path in more ways than one. It's been said the young Irish emigrant was caught in the middle, blamed for leaving his poor mother behind while grasped by wrenching homesickness even before he left.

In his passport photo he has the same haunted look that he had in the photo with his brothers.

A note - Sharing the photo of the Keane brothers with my cousins this past year, they thought it was their father, Michael, standing in the photo. From pictures I've seen, even when they were older, my dad and my Uncle Michael looked very much alike. But, I'm still of the mind it's my father. My mother told me so and she wasn't one to mince words. But considering their point of view, the historic photo now has the distinction of carrying with it the spirit of the four younger brothers, James, John, Bernard and Michael.

Barney (Brian) Keane, Detroit, Michigan
circa1930s

In this photo, my dad is in America. It's around 1938. Since immigrating to America eight years earlier, he's obviously done well for himself. He's wearing a tailored brown suit, a striped tie and high white collar. His arms are casually crossed as he leans with an air of utter confidence on the side of a classic Ford Model A. It's parked on a street in front of a white-painted house with a porch and wide front room window. It's most likely the Detroit home of his sister, Mary.

Besides leaving his home and family behind, he left his nickname Brian behind. In the States he went by Bernard, his formal name, and then simply Barney. Growing up, everyone knew him as the Irishman, Barney Keane.

In another photo my mom gave me, he appears in a U.S. military uniform with the Trident insignia for the U.S. 97th Infantry Division during WWII patched onto his left shirt sleeve.

Barney Keane joined the Army in 1943

The red and gold Thunderbird insignia depicting the Army's 45th infantry division was also among belongings passed onto my brothers Jerry and Brian. His discharge papers note that he shipped out overseas after about a year in training in the States on October 12, 1944 spending 1 year, 2 months and 23 days in combat.

It took some digging to learn more about his service, and exactly where he fought during the war. The patches, his discharge papers and a return address on letters he sent his brother, Michael, gave me clues.

Retracing my dad's footsteps

Before going back to the United States after World War II ended, my dad surprised his mom with a visit. It had been 15 years since he'd been home. When he left the second time, he promised he would be back again someday. But years went by as he made his new life in America and he never went back. My mom told me he regretted this to his dying day.

"He wanted you to go back with him," she said.

Her words haunted me. My regret put me on a path to retrace his steps that started in 2014. That's when I began traveling to Ireland every year, sometimes twice a year, until the coronavirus stopped us all in 2020.

Those trips were magical. Someone always showed up to help me on my way: my cousins Mary, Noel, Jimmy and his wonderful wife Maureen, newfound friends Jacinta Greene-Beatty, Elizabeth Kenny, Jean Higgins and Rita Morgan, and a barkeep in County Mayo when I took the wrong bus on my way to Castlerea the first time.

My dear friend Elizabeth Kenny of Roscommon Town, County Roscommon, Ireland

My dear friend Jacinta Greene-Beatty of Castlerea, County Roscommon, Ireland

Pauleen Murray of Murray's pub in Charlestown, County Mayo often helps travelers like me find their way in Ireland

I visited libraries and archives, took Irish language classes, dug up land records, learned about old Irish legends from folklorists like the most renowned and knowledgeable Daithí Ó hÓgáin, read volumes of old folk tales by William Butler Yeats, interviewed historian Jimmy Ganly, former president of the Roscommon Heritage Society and Anthony Tuohy of Castlerea and visited my cousin Noel, neighbors Finbar McNamara, James Devaney and shop owner Michael Hanly.

Along the way, I found the cemetery where my grandmother was buried, the church my grandparents were married in, the house that was home to generations of Keanes, the school my dad went to, the train station he left from and the ship he traveled to America on.

In my 60's, my dad long gone, I was just beginning to know him.

The Cottage

There was a time when my dad's brogue hung on him like a soft Irish rain. In a picture of the thatched-roof cottage he grew up in a border collie sits patiently outside the open door as if expecting someone to walk out at any moment. I like to think the dog is waiting for my dad and soon he would be walking out, and calling with a distinctive lilt in his voice, 'Come-on pup!' Like me, he loved animals. I remember how he always fed the squirrels that came up to the back door acting like pets expecting a handout.

My grandma's thatched roof cottage stood for more than 100 years

When I first saw the picture of the cottage, I didn't see the historic significance of it right away. But then, I realized it's much more than a glimpse of long-lost heritage; like other traditional structures of the past, it's a symbol of endurance and resistance. The cottage survived the Big Wind of 1839, the Protestant ascendancy, the Great Famine in the 1840s, the Rebellion of 1916 and the subsequent civil war — and so did my ancestors, who like my dad, didn't record any of it.

Going back in time

As far as I can tell, my great-grandfather, James Keane, was born around 1830 in a one-room mud structure, a typical dwelling for tenant farmers and their families at the time. The windowless structure was crowded and often filled with smoke from cooking. Usually, animals stayed inside with the family. In a story about one farmer who was asked why he kept pigs in his house, his quick reply was, "Why not, they pay the rent."

Around 1839, the Keanes of Bookalagh Townland decided it was time for a larger, more modern home. They built the cottage with the help of their neighbors who built thatched-roof cottages of their own.

"Ours was across there," said Finbar McNamara motioning to the field near the newer house he built for his family. He still lives next door to the Keanes' ancestral property with his wife Maureen.

Down Farm Road, the Devaney's cottage is still standing.

Even though he didn't speak much about his past, I think my dad fondly remembered the thatched-roof cottages up and down Farm Road with smoke billowing out of chimneys. The cottages had windows, a stove-pipe, an extra room, potato storage and a half-gate to keep the chickens and pigs out. It was a huge step up in their quality of living. Once built, the Keanes continued farming the land and getting by as best as they could.

Not long after the Keane cottage was built, the Big Wind, Oíche na Gaoithe Móire, ravaged Ireland.

My great grandfather James was around 9 years old. He might have been among the first to notice the menacing storm, because he was most likely charged with taking care of the fields, a duty of boys his age.

Based on accounts of what happened on January 6, 1839, the Big Wind obliterated everything in its path, killing hundreds of people and blowing the roofs off of thatched cottages, including my grandmother's cottage. The Big Wind was so violent some thought the end of the world had come. Once the fierce wind died down, neighbors helped each other repair their roofs, move back in and pick up on living their lives off small plots of land as they had always done.

For daily meals, families depended mostly on the potato crop, a nutritious vegetable that did well in Ireland's climate and yielded a large harvest in a small area.

One day, when James was about 15, he came in from the field and showed his mom a potato he had dug up.

"Look," he said, pointing to the smelly piece of rot in his hand.

At first, his mom thought it was a fluke. "Well, that must be an odd one, James," she surmised.

Wrapping her shawl around her shoulders, she bustled out the door before him.

Her arms began to ache, as she dug up one potato after another.

Each one had the same putrid smell of sickness.

Crossing herself, she prayed, "D'íosa, Muire, agus Seosamh sábhál-faidh sinn! (Jesus, Mary and Joseph save us!)

The fungus spread to one farm after another. The resulting famine ravaged Ireland from 1845 to 1849. One million people starved to death. One million people emigrated. Roscommon, Mayo and Galway counties in the west of Ireland were among the hardest hit.

The suffering could have been alleviated. Before and during the famine, English landlords or their agents evicted families for back rent and exported tons of food and livestock back to England.

A replica of a famine ship on the Custom House Quay in Dublin

This monument, like many around Ireland, honors famine victims who lost their lives or were forced to leave their families behind

Chapter 2 – Growing up in occupied Ireland

When my dad was born in 1908, the colonial British government was embedded in Irish society. Anglican churches loomed over towns and villages. School curriculum featured English history. Except in remote western communities, the Irish language was barely spoken anymore. Life went on in relative peace, but for Irish families there wasn't much of a future to look forward to. There were no jobs and there wasn't enough land to divide amongst all the children, so emigration was often the answer long after the Great Famine.

When he attended the national school in the Farm townland beginning around 1914, the seeds were being planted for the 1916 Rebellion.

The rebels, led by Padraig Pearse, an Irish teacher, barrister and poet, reminded the people of their colonial history and the quest for a united Ireland that had been resounding throughout the island since English occupation began 800 years ago.

I look back at the foregone past because the history lays the foundation for the events that took place in the 20th century when my dad was growing up. They tell how the British occupation dispossessed the Irish of their lands and pushed them into tenant farming at subsistence levels that offered no rights to property, availability of jobs and education.

Take a look at Henry VIII to begin with.

To gain control of Ireland, Henry set his sights on the title of King of Ireland, which the English-controlled Irish parliament agreed to, of course. History shows he didn't care about the Irish people; he was interested in gaining ground and wealth.

His daughter Queen Elizabeth I, who took the throne in 1558, didn't care much for the Irish people either. Elizabeth had the same land-grabbing intention as Henry but she also had another agenda. She had been brought up Protestant in the Church of England and felt strongly that a united religion — her religion — was the answer to just about everything.

She set out to do two things: get rid of Catholicism and take over Irish land.

To do so, Queen Elizabeth I began the system of plantations, giving Irish lands and homes to subjects loyal to the crown. Then she gave them free rein to deal with the Irish as they saw fit, which they did, turning families out of their homes, taking over their lands, then demanding they pay rent on the land taken from them. When they couldn't pay, they were thrown out of their rented property, even during the potato famine.

Parcel by parcel, ruler by ruler, the Crown continued to confiscate Irish land, passing it to loyal Protestants, mostly English or Scottish, but even some Irish.

The occupiers were called the landed gentry. They had the responsibility to build Anglican churches that everyone, Catholics included, were supposed to attend. Remains or renovations of Anglican churches are in every town throughout Ireland.

In County Roscommon's Castlerea the closest large market town to where my dad grew up in nearby County Galway, I was told Anthony Tuohy was one of the people to talk to about the history of the midlands. In his 80's, he'd been collecting historical information for decades, much of which has been preserved at the Castlerea library.

One hazy, black-and-white photo shows several stern-faced constables standing in front of a rural home by a cartload of hefty ladders that look twelve feet long.

Anthony Tuohy looks over historic papers he's collected over the years

Anthony explained that they're carrying out the landlord's edict to evict a family for failure to pay taxes imposed under British laws.

"They're getting ready to break down the house. They were very cruel," he said.

He added that when he worked in England in the 1950s, he wasn't afraid of letting the English know it wasn't right how they treated the Irish.

"I used to have it hot and heavy with the English," he declared.

A heritage organization described what typically happened. "At Carihaken, the levelers have been at work and tumbled down eighteen houses. In one of them dwelt John Killian. He told me that he and his father before him had owned this now ruined cabin for ages, and that he had paid £4 a year for four acres of ground. He owed no rent: before it was due, the landlord's drivers cut down his crops, carried them off, gave him no account of the proceeds and then tumbled his house. The old man also told me that his son having cut down a few sticks to make him a shelter, was taken up, prosecuted, and sentenced to two months confinement for destroying trees and making waste of the property." [1]

Frank Delaney, in his epic novel *Ireland*, gives another vivid description.

"It was not unusual for a stranger to knock on the door of a Catholic family and ask to see the man of the house. The stranger would tell the man, 'You have to leave this house now, for I own it. I have a piece of paper here signed by the county official that says this place has become my house and land. The man of the house would protest, 'This house and land has been in my family for centuries!'" Then, Delaney continues, the stranger whistled and redcoat soldiers with guns appeared and the family was put out on the road. Kicked out of their own homes, Delaney believes they starved to death or were sold as slaves and shipped to the West Indies.

By the mid-17th century, long after Elizabeth I was dead, 70 percent of Irish land was occupied and controlled by British loyalists who implemented laws, policies and practices discriminating against Catholics.

Some historians say there could have been a better outcome for the Irish if the Gaelic chieftains hadn't fled Ireland in September of 1607. Their departure is known as the Flight of the Earls. Among them: Hugh O'Neill, 2nd Earl of Tyrone and Rory O'Donnell, 1st Earl of Tyrconnell, and about ninety followers took off to France.

The Irish chieftains had been burning the candle at both ends, as tribal leaders of Gaelic society and as designated earls of the English-run Kingdom of Ireland. When they rebelled against their sworn allegiance to the Crown, they left Ireland for fear of being arrested for treason.

To give O'Neill and O'Donnell some slack, historical records note that they both planned to return to Ireland with their Spanish allies and reclaim their lands. But they died before they could. O'Neill died in 1616 and O'Donnell died in 1608. [2]

Before I started my research, I never knew there were so many Irish rebellions before the 1916 Rebellion or that an Irish government had formed early on.

As the oppressive British government continued its discriminatory measures and drove more and more families out of their homes, the Irish fought back.

There were the Rebellion of 1641, the Confederate wars, the Eleven-Year War, the Munster Revolt, the 9-Year War, the Williamite-Jacobite War (1689–91), the Armagh disturbances (1780s–90s) and the Irish Rebellion of 1798, to mention some.

For example, the Rebellion of 1641 started off badly on October 23 when Owen O'Connolly, a Protestant convert, turned in the leaders of the rebellion, Hugh Oge MacMahon and Conor Maguir as they attempted to take over Dublin Castle.

MacMahon's and Maguire's arrest didn't stop Phelim O'Neill and Rorry O'Moore from making claim to Derry and other northern towns, though.

O'Neill named himself king.

He was one of the first to throw off the English yoke after the Flight of the Earls. King Charles I was in power at the time.

In an effort to maintain control of his lands, O'Neill attacked a Protestant settlement, killing hundreds of English colonists in Ulster. Others followed O'Neill's charge.

Some reports say thousands of Protestants were killed in attacks and some died from the cold or disease, much like the Irish did when the English evicted them.

The English retaliated against the uprising, killing Irish civilians and prisoners at Kilwarlin Woods. At Newry, local merchants were lined up on the banks of the river and "butchered to death ... without any legal process."

"Then the MacDonald clan was attacked and the women thrown over the cliffs to their deaths on rocks below." [3.] Catholics fought back again in Portadown, Kilmore and Shrule, to name some. The killings committed by both sides rooted the division between Catholics and Protestants.

After the Rebellion of 1641, the Irish Catholic upper classes and clergy formed the **Catholic Confederation in May, 1642.** The Confederation became a de facto government, free from the control of the English administration.

The Confederation held on to Irish independence and governance until 1649. That's when England sent in Oliver Cromwell's New Model Army to end the uprisings once and for all, which he did through terror and violence. With 20,000 troops marching on Drogheda and Wexford, the British slaughtered everyone in sight, women and children included. Those who weren't killed were enslaved and never seen again.

Claiming victory over the Irish, the English Parliament announced the terms of surrender, which resulted in the mass confiscation of pretty much all the rest of Irish land. With most of the land occupied, oppression towards Irish Catholics became the letter of the law.

In 1690, Protestant King William of Orange claimed victory over Catholic King James during the Battle of Boyne, then William rolled out the penal laws. Delaney writes that the penal laws were also known as the "popery laws," because they were designed to remove all power and influence from the Catholic population.

Under the penal laws, Catholics couldn't own a horse worth more than five pounds, run for an elected office, work in government, become a lawyer, buy or lease land, open a shop, live in town, vote, carry a gun, speak Irish or practice the Catholic religion.

The British law required all Catholic priests and bishops to leave Ireland. If they didn't leave, they risked being branded and shot or drawn and quartered. Teachers were also targets. Both went underground, priests holding Mass outdoors and teachers setting up what was known as "hedge schools" where classes were taught out of sight in the dugout foliage of roadside hedges. For safety, they were often moved to different locations.

On a visit to Ballaghadereen in County Mayo, Mike Carty, a local tour guide took me to the hillside where an ancient outdoor chapel still stands. The chapel has four sides so the priest could administer the sacraments from any direction. Each side has a cubicle and ledge to hold a chalice and from each vantage point, he could see for miles.

This ancient Catholic chapel called the Four Altars was used in Ireland at a time when Catholicism was banned in the country

Here, I'm standing in the interior of one of the four sides of the Four Altars. It's about 5 km from Ballaghadereen on the main Sligo Road

From where I stood on the hillside in one of the alters, I imagined the priest hurriedly packing up the chalice and he and others riding away as fast as they could when they saw the British charging their way.

One day, James Devaney, who grew up in Bookalagh around the same time I was growing up in the States, took me on a drive around the townland and the village of Ballymoe. Turning on to Farm Road, he pointed to a clump of bushes not far from where my grandma's cottage once stood.

"Right there was a hedge school," he pointed out.

The reference point put another historical marker in sequence for me. It was the first time I'd thought back to the time of my great-great-grandfather, who he was and what he experienced. With James Keane being born around 1830, his father, my great-great-grandfather, would have been born in the late 1700s or early 1800s and most likely attended a hedge school during the time penal laws were being carried out.

Chapter 3 –
Colonial Cruelty

Colonialism, wherever it takes over the land and its people, has similar tactics - violence, occupation, domination — sending children to boarding schools, glorifying colonists, evictions, murdered and missing women and stripping away land, language and traditional practices.

While colonialism is known as the Protestant Ascendency in Ireland, the push to take over tribal lands in the States is known as Manifest Destiny.

As Ireland was called "the Irish problem" by the British, the U.S. called Tribal Nations the "Indian Problem". The U.S. and England handled the "problems" the same way – with brutal, inhumane violence.

In *Indigenous Voices of the Colorado Plateau*[4], General James Henry Carleton is identified as the head of the forced relocation operation of the Navajo people who live in the mountains of Utah, Arizona and New Mexico. He used Manifest Destiny as his mantra to take over tribal land and strip indigenous people of their culture and language.

To carry out his vision, in 1864, Carleton ordered Christopher (Kit) Carson to defeat the Navajo (Diné) resistance by conducting a scorched-earth campaign across the Diné homelands. Carson burned villages, slaughtered livestock, and destroyed water sources.

Then they were forced by gunpoint to march on the "Long Walk" in the dead of winter between 250 and 450 miles to a concentration camp in

Ft. Sumner, New Mexico. To the Diné it is known as Hweeldi. Hundreds of the people died along the way, many elders, women and children. Those who couldn't keep up were shot. In 1868, the Navajos were released and they made their way home to Dinétah, their homeland.

The comparative history between the colonial cruelty of the U.S. on Native peoples and the British on the Irish is illustrated in works of art by Navajo weaver and quilter Susan Hudson and Irish fibre artist Frances Crowe.

Navajo fabric artist Susan Hudson points out scenes in her quilted tapestry depicting the final harsh years at Hweeldi.*

*Irish fabric artist Frances Crowe stands by "Displaced," her woven portrayal of Irish famine refugees alongside Syrian refugees fleeing their war-torn country ***

While Hudson and Crowe live and work on different sides of the Atlantic Ocean, their narrative art portrays the aftermath of colonization and genocide that's left homes and families in ruins around the world.

Hudson's story-telling quilts depict the life of her people during their years of captivity at Hweeldi. She said the buyer of one of her tapestries survived the German concentration camp Auschwitz during WWII where hundreds of thousands of Jewish people died horrendous deaths at the hands of Nazi soldiers.

"When he looked at it, what grabbed his heart is, 'You can change the clothing, you can change their uniform, and it would be what I went through,'" she recalled him saying.

Depicted on one quilted panel are haunting images of children begging for food, wilting crops, turned-over crosses paying tribute to those who died, and an upside-down American flag protesting the U.S. government's inhumane treatment of American Indians.

"Right here, I'm showing how these soldiers had so much power to do anything they wanted to a person. They could kill them, beat them, rape them, sell them, and nothing was going to happen to them. They would get away literally with murder," she said, her voice rising.

Turning to another section of her wall-sized quilted story, Hudson said, "This is year three and year four. This is when they're really starving. They're trying to grow crops, but the crops are failing."

Observing the details, Ezekiel Argeanas, Diné, added, "Their hearts are broken because they don't know what to do. It is a holocaust we are looking at in this piece."

Crowe, from Ireland's County Roscommon, tells similar stories of forced exodus on her sweeping scenic tapestry "Displaced," depicting the Irish who were driven off their lands fleeing hunger and starvation during the mid-1800s. Alongside them, Syrian families fleeing violence in their war-torn country in more recent times.

Crowe said she was inspired to tell the story of Syrian refugees along with the story of the Irish famine, because like the Irish, Syrian families lost so many of their loved ones.

Cynthia Cook, a distinguished New Mexico mixed media artist defines an artist as one who manifests love in their work.

"Crowe's tapestry succeeds monumentally on this level and beyond," she said.

"Her work is testimony to the patience it takes to assist with healing. Weaving a large piece indicates a daily meditative, prayer-like process, a spell-like invocation of hope," she added. [5, 6, 7, 8, 9]

Chapter 4 –
Resilience & Resistance

Ancestors of Cromwell's soldiers were among the loyalists who received titles to Irish land. One of them was Theophilus Sandford, who took over lands that included the town of Castlerea and the estate of the Clan O'Conor, the last of the Irish High Kings. My grandmother Bridget Connor traced her heritage back to the O'Conor clan.

When Sandford moved in, he built an estate in the demesne, a spacious open area with rolling hills, woods and a stream running through it. He also had an Anglican church built on the highest eastern hill of the town where the bishop could look out on the townspeople and keep an eye on them.

As the bishop stood unseen in the towering stone edifice, townspeople, mostly Catholic, went about their business, they were undoubtedly aware of the watchful eyes of their occupiers.

British constables and tax collectors kept a close eye on the citizenry, too.

"Land agents collected rent for the landlords, (most of whom were absentee, living in Dublin or London)," explained historian Jimmy Ganly.

Similar to Native American lands, where few businesses operate and most money is spent outside of tribal lands, Ireland was a poor country at the time.

"A lot of the wealth was sent out of the country — cash, corn, cattle and sheep," Ganly added.

It's been said that the blight that lasted four years killed the crop; indifference killed the Irish people.

The exportation of food and supplies continued throughout the famine.

My great-grandfather James and his family and others in nearby townlands on occasion took a horse and cart to Castlerea for supplies that weren't available in the nearby village of Ballymoe.

While there, they drove by the lavish Sandford Estate and were reminded of the extreme disparity between their family's way of life and the luxurious lifestyle of the Protestant overseers. They accepted it as their lot in life, but prayed for the day when the English were expelled and the Irish got their land back. [10.]

They also passed by the workhouse, which began to be built around 1838. Also known as the poorhouse, it was said to be England's failed solution to overwhelming poverty in Ireland. Seeing the cold, stone building, chills went down their backs. If they fell on bad times, they could end up there, separated from their families and most likely never to return home.

"You would be giving up what little land you had and your house and put yourself at the mercy of the workhouse. The father would be separated from his wife and children. They would be given menial jobs to do," noted Ganly.

The workhouse system ended around 1920.

But, there were landlords who watched out for their Irish tenants.

"Some were good and looked after the people who were starving and the (landlords) suffered financially for it. During the famine, they mortgaged their homes and land to pay for soup kitchens or they might not take rent off people for a couple of years, which meant they were losing money," explained Ganly.

The landlord over the Ballymoe Barony, which included Bookalagh and the surrounding areas, was Thomas H. Burke. As part of English occupation, he was given 25,000 acres with a mansion and demesne at Marble Hill, Loughrea, according to the thesis, *The Impact of the Wyndham Land Act 1903 on County Galway* by Tom Tonge.[11]

Burke is referred to as a handsome and genial type of guy.

Unlike most landlords, who were English or Scottish, he was Irish. He may have inherited or received his estate in exchange for services to the Crown, or possibly through marriage. Burke married Lady Mary Nugent, daughter of Anthony Nugent, 9th Earl of Westmeath. Burke also had a position on the British parliament.

Perhaps Burke was one of the landlords that helped families living on his estate during the famine. This seems to be the case since in 1856, the Keane cottage and shed were still standing, along with a cottier, a small cottage for a hired worker and his family.

My great-great grandfather must have passed away by then, because James Keane's name is listed on the 1856 land record for one acre, three roods, and 20 perches. There are four roods in an acre, and in turn a rood contains 40 perches.

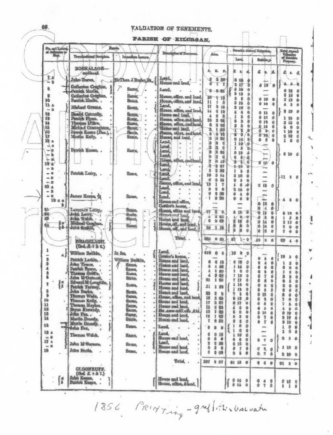

Copyright All rights reserved

1856 Printing - gryffith valuation

These entries in the 1856 printing of the Griffith's Valuation of Tenements shows that James Keane was renting less than two acres of land from Sir Thomas J. Burke

Surviving the Famine

My great-grandfather James married Margaret Raftery from County Roscommon most likely around the time the land passed to him.

"It wouldn't necessarily have been about love, more about survival. She would have had a dowry," explained Eileen Finnegan of Williamstown, a member of the Williamstown Heritage Society of County Galway.

To learn more about the landlord/tenant relationship, historian Jimmy Ganly, the former president of the Roscommon Historical Society, agreed to an interview. Jacinta invited us to have the meeting at her house.

Jimmy brought with him an armful of books and a briefcase stuffed with files. Jacinta greeted us warmly and showed us to the spacious dining room table where Jimmy pulled out reports, maps, studies and diagrams.

Historian Jimmy Ganly shares knowledge about the history of Ireland's midlands

Soon after we sat down Jimmy stressed that the most important aspect to know about occupation is how the land is divided up in the first place.

In Ireland, the government targeted existing homesites and labeled the smallest division as the "townland". It was originally based on "bally-boes", areas of land deemed sufficient to sustain a cow. Over time, townlands of varying sizes were established and by the 1830s there were some townlands of less than one acre and others of several thousand acres. Land was rented out using the name of the townland and they were used as a basis of census returns. Beyond the townland, there's the city and town, the diocese, parish, barony and county.[12]

Explaining the history of plotting land in Ireland, Ganly told how the British hired surveyors to determine who lived where, how much land they lived on, what kind of structures were on the land and the size and number of windows. Measuring land and the dwellings on it - is the key to ownership and taxation; it's a very ancient concept, according to locista.com.

The taxation scheme explained my grandmother's tiny windows. The larger the windows, the more the tax. Same with improvements. If the family had made changes to the house or land, they would be charged extra for that as well.

Jimmy said an early census taker who worked under contract with the British government was a man called John O'Donovan.

"He would stay with the landlord, have a good accommodation, access to a library and get information from the church," he explained.

"Then, he would spend his day walking the land or riding horseback, taking copious notes. Once he visited all the houses in area, which may have consisted of several farms, he'd let the British Army know and they would come to map the area," he continued.

"This was around 1836 and1837; that was when the first map was made," Jimmy said.

In the States, the federal government relocated tribal nations to reservations mostly on stark land with minimal water resources.

Around noon, when her husband, Ciaran, came home for lunch, Jacinta served a traditional Irish dinner, plates of pork ribs that melted off the rack, steamed cabbage and traditional oven bread.

It was the best lunch ever!

Great-grandparents

James and Margaret had four children, according to a historical ancestral report my brother Brian gave me: my grandfather Bernard around 1864, Margaret, 1865; James 1868; and Honor 1870.

My grandfather, Bernard, married Bridget Connor also of Bookalagh on February 5, 1894. I gather he was around 30 years old.

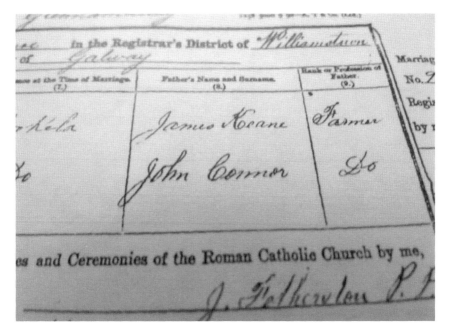

Great grandfathers James Keane and John Connor witness the marriage of Bernard Keane and Bridget Connor

Since there's no record of that day except its date on a census record, I imagine it went like this.

On the day of the wedding, Bernard dressed in his one best Sunday suit.

His parents, James and Margaret, were already dressed and waiting for him outside the cottage where they had readied a horse and cart.

When Bernard appeared, they greeted him, complimenting him on his fine looks. On the way to the church, they were quiet, each thinking how life was about to change with the newlyweds and the prospect of having grandchildren. Slowly driving to St. Croan's church in Ballymoe, they arrived just as the bells were announcing the wedding ceremony was about to begin.

Bridget was already at the church. She was 24.

Based on the record of marriage, Bridget's parents were John Connor and Honor (Kearns) Connor. John Flanagan and Katie Kearns, most likely Bridget's sister, witnessed Bernard and Bridget's marriage. The newlywed couple settled down with my great grandparents in the cottage that survived the big wind, the famine and evictions.

In the 1901 census record my great-grandmother Margaret was living with them still. She's noted as being a widow and an Irish and English speaker, aged 61.

1901 Irish Census

Altogether, the 1901 census lists my grandparents Bernard and Bridget, my great grandmother Margaret, Mary, James and the youngest child Bridget, around one year old.

Life went on as usual as the family made a subsistence living off the small piece of land – less than two acres — taking care of a few animals and a field of potatoes and other vegetables and fruits, while paying rent to the landlord.

The land record notes that James annually owed 4 pounds, 5 shillings, for property and the buildings. The family may have paid with a portion of what they grew and the animals they raised.

1911 Census

By the next census in 1911, my great-grandmother had passed away. According to her death certificate, she died on July 27, 1910 "probably of bronchitis." My grandmother Bridget was by her side. The child Bridget's name is also missing on the 1911 census.

The family now consisted of my grandma and grandpa, Mary, James, Delia, Patrick, Celia, my dad Bernard and John. Mary was born in 1895, James 1897, Delia 1901, Patrick 1904, Celia 1906, Bernard 1908, John 1911. Michael was born in 1914.

From left to right, Uncle Michael, Aunt Celia, Aunt Delia

On my last visit with Finbar in 2019, he talked about the early land conflict, called the "Irish Question" in Britain and "Land Wars" in Ireland.

The Irish National Land League, Conradh na Talún, was organized in October of 1878. Its purpose was to diminish the unaffordable rents and help Irish farmers own the land they worked on. Through the group's agitation, they aimed to abolish the landlord system.

"The land of Ireland, for the people of Ireland," was their slogan.

"It's all about land," said Jacinta during one of our many get-togethers for coffee or tea.

Women played a significant role. The Ladies' Land League started in 1881. Finbar expressed dismay that their valiant and heroic efforts have seldom been acknowledged.

"In the 1880s, many of the men were put into prison for agitating (the British government). The women stepped in. They became political a long time before they were allowed to vote," Finbar, who was well read in Irish history, noted.

Women didn't get the right to vote in Ireland until 1922.

"They got sympathy from all around the country and plenty of publicity and shame on the landlords," Finbar said.

In 1844, a future British prime minister, Benjamin Disraeli, defined the Irish Question:

"A dense population, in extreme distress, inhabit an island where there is an established church, which is not their Church, and a territorial aristocracy the richest of whom live in foreign capitals. Thus, you have a starving population, an absentee aristocracy, and an alien Church; and in addition, the weakest executive in the world. That is the Irish Question."

Then, due to the building political pressure, things began to change.

Finbar brought my attention to laws that were passed early on that set the stage for Ireland to regain its land back from under British control.

The Encumbered Estates Acts, Land Act, Arrears Act, and the Wyndham Land Purchase Act passed between 1881 and 1903.

The Land Act of 1903 allowed tenant farmers to buy their land with a long-term government loan through the Land Commission.

"They could have 68-and-a-half years, more than a generation. It was painless, they didn't have to pay vast sums of money and they had enough money to keep the farm going. They were paying the Irish Land Commission at this time. Because of the affordable payback scheme, it was referred to as 'paying back on the drip,'" said Ganly.

In 1903, five years before my dad was born, the Wyndham Land Purchase Act was passed, which began the breakdown of large landlord estates. In Castlerea, the Sandford estate, called the Castlereagh House, was torn down after Irish independence. Today, all that's left is the gates.

In 1903, Irish property records show James Keane's name crossed off and my grandfather Bernard Keane Sr.'s name inserted. He owned 20 acres, 1 rood and 1 pence of land, having gained 19 acres since 1856 — most likely from the 19th century land laws.

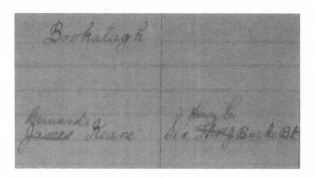

Irish Land entry - 1903

On the same land record, Sir Henry Thomas Burke's name is crossed off, indicating that he also had died by this time. Henry G. Burke's name is inserted, but unlike his predecessor, he didn't have the same role as a landlord because of the land laws, so he may have sold off his interest and pulled up stakes soon after. Under the new land laws, landlords were given a 12% bonus for selling their whole estate. It's said that most jumped at the chance since they were having a hard time making ends meet with defaults rising on debts and rents, and they feared the political hostility that was rising up against them.

With the land ownership finally in his hands, Bernard Sr., my grandfather, most likely began the process of paying his mortgage. The 1903 record shows his debt cost six pounds, ten shillings for the land, and 15 shillings for the buildings: the cottage, the cottier and the shed, yearly.

By 1914, about 80% of Irish tenants had purchased their holdings. [13.]

In 1951, I was two years old when my grandmother passed away. She was 80. My dad never mentioned the elaborate sending-off his mom probably had in Ireland; the laying out in the house where everyone for miles would come to pay their respects; the rosary and songs, then a Mass the next day, followed by a solemn procession to her burial place in the Kilcroan cemetery where the priest said more prayers until her coffin was covered with special mementos from loved ones and finally sprinkled with holy water and covered with dirt that the priest had blessed. Then the whole congregation, including the priest, would go to a pub in Ballymoe, eat, drink and tell stories about all she had done in her lifetime.

Seeing a photo of her for the first time, I wondered even more about who she was, how she dealt with her son leaving and how she looked forward to him coming home one day again, as he promised. While it's hard to tell the color of her hair in the black and white photo, my grandma's hair has a soft hue to it, which makes me think it was auburn. My dad, who had black hair, took after his father.

Next to her in the picture is one of her sisters, either Cecelia Mitchel or Nora Scahill.

On the left, Bridget Connor Keane, my grandmother.
Sitting next to her is her sister Celia Mitchell or sister Nora Scahill

Chapter 5 –
Bookalagh

An engraved stone marks the townland of Bookalagh

Finbar McNamara, my dad's neighbor, remembered my grandma well.

He was born in 1934. She would have been in her 60s. He grew up knowing her until she passed away.

"Your grandmother, Bridget, was a Connor from the O'Conor clan, the high chieftains of Ireland. They were very educated and talented," he recalled.

Finbar was 82 when I first interviewed him in 2015. He reminded me of my dad. He had kind, sensitive eyes and a warm smile that made me feel welcome. He, like my dad, worked hard all his life for his family.

"She was a great woman, a very bright woman. She took on all the responsibilities of raising crops, making sure the peat was cut, taking care of the cattle and (horse) and cooking traditional dishes like bacon, cabbage and potatoes," Finbar continued.

He commended her for doing it all alone after my grandpa passed away in 1924.

Finbar said my grandma was especially clever. Whenever she had a chance, she found ways to bring income into the family, like raising ducks instead of chickens.

"They got a better price on duck eggs than chicken eggs. They had a big range of ducks – 50 to 60, and they would lay an egg a day. Every morning, they waddled down near our house; you could hear them quacking on the way to the river," he recalled.

My grandma also provided traditional services at funerals. She was a keener, my cousin Noel told me over dinner one night at Gleeson's restaurant in Roscommon Town.

As was the practice of keening, when she was invited into a home after a death, she put on a dark shawl, sat in full view of everyone near the departed loved one and expressed from the deep core of her being, in bone-chilling cries, their sadness.

Keening was a common Irish practice until it died out Some point fingers at British interference in traditional practices, others say it was Catholic priests, according to a presentation on how the keening tradition died out at Irish funerals posted at IrishCentral.com.

Noel also said she was a healer with knowledge of bone setting and herbal remedies.

My daughter Joanna took after her, learning herbal arts and medicines. She is also preserving traditional structures. She is an enjaradora, a traditional woman mud plasterer.

About her work, Joanna writes, "We practice traditions to reconnect with our natural identities. When an older woman teaches a younger woman to master a traditional craft, the younger woman gains a piece of the past, and brings it with her to the present. As we walk the same paths and repeat the same gestures as our ancestors, we travel through time."

While Joanna works with adobe, a southwestern material used in home building by her ancestors on her father's side, she also has an appreciation of the traditional construction materials and resiliency of her great-grandmother's cottage in Ireland.

The Cottage

Finbar remembered the cottage well before it was torn down after my grandma's passing.

A closer look at the Keane cottage shows the roof was in the process of being re-thatched

"(The cottage) was nicely set up. It was built with a window and a full view of the road. It was made from mud with bog dale timber and thatched materials for the roof. It had a stone floor in the kitchen and two rooms. There was a pole in the center of the front room to fortify the roof," he said.

In his book *Ballymoe*, John Brady [14] describes four classes of houses in Ireland: one-room windowless structures; the cottage with windows and rooms, like my grandmother's was a 3rd class house; 2nd class was a good farm house; and a house with five to nine windows, a 1st class house.

A picture of a Keane house stood out for me in Brady's book.

Keane House and Household, Bookalagh, c. 1900

One of three Keane families living in Bookalagh in 1900 pictured in John Brady's book Ballymoe

On a visit to John Brady's home in Ballymoe, I asked John if it might be my family. He said, "No, that's not Bernard Keane's place." There were three Keanes that lived in Bookalagh at the time, and not related, he added.

The cottage was similar though, Mrs. Brady pointed out.

"There would have been a big open fire in the living room. In addition to the two rooms, there may have been a loft, or a mezzanine and somewhere in the house would be a storage room for potatoes," she said.

"Before the fireplace there was a hearth stone. Neighbors would gather at night around the fire; that is how news was spread and shared. They cooked and baked on an open fire," she added.

The third, similar, cottage on Farm Road belonged to the Devaneys. I imagined James, who was around my age, walking to school and back every day passing my grandma's house as he went and Meadow, my dad's dog, followed him chasing the ducks on the way to river before turning back to go home.

As country neighbors, the Keanes, McNamaras and Devaneys helped each other out with planting, harvesting, cutting peat and traditional health care.

"Those were happy days," Finbar said.

Finbar remembered my aunts and uncles fondly, too. They were around 15 to 20 years older than he.

"I learned a lot from John Keane. He was enterprising. Lovely job on everything. He was brilliant. (For example), when John thatched the roof, he did a lovely job and he was a great plow man. He'd follow the lead with the horses," Finbar said.

He recalled how precise he was during harvest time.

Maureen and Finbar McNamara live down the road from the Keanes' ancestral land.
Finbar shared memories of my dad, grandma, aunts and uncles

Uncle John was known for being one of the best farmers around

"We used to (cut) the oats and bind them into sheaves and then make stokes tying ten or twelve sheaves together. They'd be left to dry out. His row of sheaves would also be dead straight.

"Celia was a mother to me, aye she was. She was very lovely. We worked together plowing the fields with the horses. Between the two houses, we had a horse each," Finbar continued.

"Michael was a blacksmith. The jobs he did were fantastic. He was very artistic."

On my visit to the Bradys, Mrs. Brady walked with me outside to show me one of my Uncle Michael's many handcrafted pieces throughout the countryside, a sturdy metal gate.

Mrs. John Brady stands by a well-crafted gate to the entrance of her home in Ballymoe. It was designed and constructed by my Uncle Michael, the town's blacksmith

Noted Ganly, "The local blacksmith would be a very important man. He'd make shoes for horses and donkeys, hinges for doors, nails for the carpenter; just about anything that was made from metal, he could make it, even the crane that held the pots and pans over the open fire, he would make those."

Michael Hanly of Drimatemple also remembered my Uncle Michael.

Michael greeted me with a wide smile as I walked into Star Trophies, a business he started with his son. In his 80s, Michael appears 20 years younger, bubbling over with a bundle of joy that seemed to fill the room. Looking around at the shelves of trophies that line the room, he said proudly, "My son does the assembly work."

*James Devaney (Lf) and Michael Hanly (Rt) pose for a photo
in Michael's trophy shop near Ballymoe*

Remembering my Uncle Michael, he said, "My father would send me with a pony or horse to your Uncle Michael's forge in Ballymoe. He was very good, very thorough at metal work. We looked up to him," he said adding that in addition to being the local blacksmith, Uncle Michael started a dancehall in Ballinlough.

"We used to go to the hall there, the Shamrock Ballroom," he recalled.

My Uncle Michael also sold religious goods on Sundays at Knock, the site of a Catholic shrine that draws a half a million people a year who pay tribute to the Blessed Virgin Mary who appeared to several young children there on August 21,1879.

"There were scapulars, rosary beads, holy pictures, holy water bottles, little crosses that you could look through them and see a representation of the apparition, all that type of goods.

He was a hard worker, he wasn't afraid. No-one else would chance (new adventures like that)," he added.

My brother Brian and Uncle Michael at his home in Ballymoe around 2001

Michael Hanly remembered my Uncle James.

"That would be him, yes," he agreed, referring to the young man with striking eyes in the Dublin photo of the Keane brothers.

Uncle James was known for his creative talent

"We used to have a dramatic society. James was good at producing plays."

The society practiced in halls in Ballymoe and Ballintubber, continued Michael thoughtfully.

"James would come in, direct us and give us information on what to do," he added.

The drama group staged three-act plays, many of them dramatic performances about Irish resistance, like "He Died for Ireland," and others about the rebellion and civil war.

"And, we did comedy. It was something to do during the long winter's nights," Michael remembered fondly.

The plays did something else: they brought people together from Galway and Roscommon counties.

"On the most part, Roscommon folks kept to themselves and the Galway folks kept to themselves. Even at church. Galway people would stay at the far side of the church, Roscommon the other side. They wouldn't intermix, except Bookalagh folks, who were from Galway County. They would side more with Roscommon", Michael explained.

"That is how we started the drama club," he said with a smile.

One day in January of 2020 just before I left to go back to the States, Rita Morgan and I took a drive to Bookalagh to take another look at where my dad grew up. We stopped at the Devaney cottage.

Noticing us, a lady walked out to say "Hello" and see what we were about.

She recognized Rita right away from attending a class together. Rita introduced Ismelda to me and she immediately phoned up her brother-in-law, James Devaney, to let him know one of the Keanes had come around.

On a day soon after, James took me on a ride through Bookalagh and Ballymoe.

This stone monument welcomes visitors to Ballymoe

On the drive down Farm Road, we passed the Kellys, Finnegans, Connaughtons, Fannons, Eagons, Doyles, my Uncle John's new house, the Keane ancestral land where my grandmother's cottage once stood, the McNamaras, and many others who had made their home close to where County Galway and County Roscommon meet.

"That's John Burn's place, a bachelor. There's a lot of history of bachelors in the west of Ireland," he mentioned.

"The next house is the Wards. Jimmy Ward has lived here for 30 years, fabulous carpenter. On the left is Finbar's daughter's house, and that was the Caseys," he said, referring to a house close by with red and yellow-framed windows.

"They've been there for a few generations," he said.

As we came up the main road, James pointed out the landscape.

"As you can see the land is very poor quality. When there's a heavy rain, it gets flooded easily," he noted as we made our way into Ballymoe, passing a small café and a hair salon.

"We are coming up to what used to be Connaughton's butcher shop. Johnny Connaughton took over the shop and later his daughter Ann turned it into an antique shop."

Then he pointed out the poet John Walsh's house.

"John went to America with Father Flannagan and we lost track of him. He wrote some nice poems," he recalled.

"And there's Pat Scahill's place, who would have been related to yourself, Colleen. They would be the same Scahills that have the shops in Castlerea on St. Patrick Street.

"That's Dominique O'Connor's shop on the right. He used to fix bicycles and he had a little garage there for repair work," he added.

On our way out of Ballymoe, we passed the Catholic Church where my grandparents were married and the house where the freedom fighter Eamonn Ceannt was born.

"His father came up here as an RIC (Royal Irish Constabulary) man, then moved the family to Dublin," James said filling in some history.

This dedication to Eamonn Ceannt, one of the courageous Irish freedom fighters, stands in a memorial garden in Ballymoe

Eamonn Ceannt lived here on the road into Ballymoe

Although James was from County Galway, he went to school in Drimatemple across the River Suck in County Roscommon. The mix of County Roscommon and County Galway kids at the school is probably another reason why Bookalagh youth got along on both sides of the River Suck.

But my dad never mentioned County Roscommon; he'd only say he was from County Galway. So, maybe the camaraderie between Roscommon and Galway folks didn't get underway until after he left for America.

Pointing out an aging single-story school building, James said he and his classmates walked there every day from Bookalagh.

"It's about four miles one way to walk," James recalled.

His teachers were Mrs. Farrell and Mrs. Kennedy who lives in Ballymoe. The headmaster was Seamus Carny.

On our roundabout, we also stopped at the old estate of the aristocrat Blake Kelly, now owned by Gerry Griffin and his wife.

James Devaney (Lf) and Gerry Griffin (Rt)

"Blake Kelly was the local landlord. He was the landed gentry, old money," James noted.

On our visit, Gerry showed us around the estate, the main house, stables and sheds. I imagined the bustling life of the landlord with carriages driving up on certain nights, the door wide open to receive well-to-do guests in tuxes and evening gowns in the styles of the time.

The old Blake Kelly Estate is now the home of an Irish family

Chapter 6 -
School under British rule

I always thought my dad was brought up speaking Irish. Surprised I would think that Finbar said, "Oh no, we all spoke English by that time."

One Irish writer wrote, "Irish had been beaten out of the country."

Under the penal laws of the 1600s, the Irish language was banned. But many Irish still spoke Gaelic fluently up until the mid-1800s. That's when England introduced a national education system. To make sure Irish children began using the Queen's language, the schools introduced the tally stick, bata scoir, to parents.

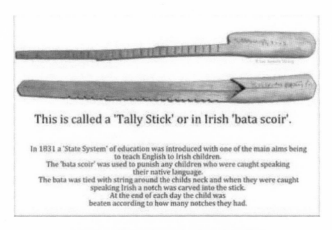

This is called a 'Tally Stick' or in Irish 'bata scoir'.

In 1831 a 'State System' of education was introduced with one of the main aims being to teach English to Irish children.
The 'bata scoir' was used to punish any children who were caught speaking their native language.
The bata was tied with string around the childs neck and when they were caught speaking Irish a notch was carved into the stick.
At the end of each day the child was beaten according to how many notches they had.

During late 18th and early 19th century the tally stick
was used to keep children from speaking Irish

Educators under British rule argued that it was in the child's best interest to leave the old language behind and learn English, so that Irish children would have opportunities in the wider society.

This was often the same thinking passed along to Native American parents who were encouraged to have their children learn English and not pass along their indigenous languages.

According to some sources, many Irish parents agreed to use the tally stick on their children. The child wore the stick on a rope around their neck. At home, whenever they spoke a word of Irish, the parent would put a notch in the stick. The next day, the teacher would collect the sticks and for each notch the child would be hit. [15.]

Around the turn of the 20th century, the only people speaking Irish to any degree were the people in the west of Ireland in Galway, Roscommon and Mayo counties. Notations on the 1901 census state that the last person in my family to speak Irish fluently was my great-grandmother, Margaret Raftery from County Roscommon.

By the time my dad went to school when he was around six years old in 1914, English was the predominantly spoken language in Ireland.

"When you went to school in those days you were under British rule," explained Jimmy Ganly.

The school my dad attended was in the Farm townland about two miles from Bookalagh.

Closing in the 1970s, the Farm School was originally a school under British administration until Ireland gained its independence

If my dad and his brothers and sisters weren't needed at home, they walked there every day. They most likely brought with them pieces of coal or turf as part of the cost of their education. They may have worn tally sticks that were still in use until around the 1920s.

"The students were taught a British curriculum. They wouldn't have learned about their own history, they would have learned about English history, unless the school master was a keen Republican," Ganly pointed out.

Writing about education in 1916, Emma Dineen, president of the Irish National Teachers' Organization (INTO), said Irish schools were seriously underfunded since government resources were being diverted to World War I. So, parents were expected to pay for supplies.

But Dineen explained, "Most parents could contribute little more than a sod or turf for the fire."

"Often there wasn't even funds for paper and pencils, so students were required to memorize their lessons by heart and orally report on them, instead of writing them down," she wrote.

This still seemed to be the case when Finbar McNamara and Padraig Beatty went to school.

On one visit, Finbar burst out in a poem about Ballymoe, reciting verses by heart.

The Boy from Marnell's Grove
by John J. Walsh recited by Finbar McNamara

A boy with the dreams of a man was he,

A man from a lonesome place

And he turned away from his family,

The width of the world to face,

Light of pocket, but heavy of heart,

He started from Marnell's Grove

And his soul grew sick as he paused to part from the

Meadows he used to roam.

He set his bundle by the side of the road

And looked with a sob of pain

On the Bookalagh River, and all abroad

That he may never see again.

Then plucking a primrose from the hedge

For spring was green on the sod.

He faired away in his wanderings,

His fate in the hands of God.

Oh, many a tear did his mother shed

In rosaries said for him,

And his father's sorrows grew broad and deep

From eyes that were growing dim;

But, the boy who started from Marnell's Grove,

He was out in the world of men,

Seeking the wealth in a far-off town

That would carry him home again.

Then when the head of him was white,

And the step of him faint and slow,

Said he, it's back by the morning's light

To the home of my youth, I'll go;

Though my parents both in the graveyard be,

And the noon of my life is set,

Sure "Marnell's Grove is the same" said he, and "The river is running yet."

He journeyed back from the world of men,

And the heart of him leaped with joy

To see again the Bookalagh River

And the fields he roamed as a boy.

Ninety-year-old Padraig Beatty also remembered a song from his younger days, and sang it to me over the phone from his home in Castlerea.

"In the county of Roscommon through the hills on that way, I was crossing the fields on my way to a train. I met a colleen and do you know, she says there's a cutting to our Ballymoe. 'I think I will go with you to show you the way,'" he sang melodically.

Besides learning poems and songs by heart and not having pen nor paper much of the time, students were immersed in history — that is, English history. To emphasize England's position in the world, Ganly said most British-run, English-only schools posted a map of the world in the center of the classroom highlighting the British Empire in red.

Penmanship must have been high on the list of educational accomplishments. My dad's handwriting, both script and blocked capital words, was impeccable, easy to read as typewritten words and evenly spaced.

Minus Irish history and culture, Leo Finnegan, the last schoolteacher at the Farm School before it closed down in the 1970s and chairman of the Williamstown Heritage Society, said the students received a good, rounded education.

"They were not just the basics, but also the classics, and even a little bit of Shakespeare," he said.

I first met Leo in November, 2016 taking a taxi to Williamstown from Castlerea where I was staying at Rita's bed and breakfast, Arm Cashel.

Leo Finnegan was the last teacher who taught at the Farm School

The taxi driver dropped me off at the square in Williamstown. I had no idea where Leo lived but I expected anyone in town would know. So, I walked down the road to see if I could find his house. It was only a matter of minutes before a gentleman stopped and asked who I was looking for. He pointed to a bungalow up the road.

"That's where you will find him," he said with a smile.

Leo opened the door and directed me to a sitting room where he explained the changing history of the school.

The Farm School was one of thousands included in a British school system under England's National Education Act of 1831. It took a while for schools to be built around Ireland though. He said, with the help of Henry Burke, referring most likely to the landlord at that time, the two-room schoolhouse was built around 1870.

Leo said that John Haveren from Dunmore, Liam Costello from County Galway and then Tom O'Donnell from Castlebar in County Mayo taught at the school.

"Your dad probably was taught by him (O'Donnell)," Leo suggested. He said at the time there was a dwelling next to the school where O'Donnell had lived.

Leo Finnegan taught at the Farm School from 1965 until the school closed in 1974. Students were transferred to more centralized schools in Williamstown and Castlerea.

"That was an end of an era really because when an area loses a school, it loses a big part of its identity," Leo lamented.

Etched into the front of the school building is the date 1928, which most likely refers to the date when the school opened its doors under the newly established Irish government after the War of Independence, erasing the previous British history.

But, Leo added, the history of English administration shouldn't be forgotten,

"It's a big loss to the community. The school served Farm and Bookalagh children for 104 years from 1870 to 1974," he said.

In 2016, Mary Cuffe of Ballymoe learned about my interest in the school and offered to take me out to see it.

The building is still standing but it's quite dilapidated. People hung out there over time and left their garbage behind; the surrounding area is overgrown with weeds and foliage making it difficult to walk around the building. Windows are broken and doors askew.

When I brought the subject up as part of a presentation at the Tarmon National School in Castlerea, a student said, "That's awful."

I agreed with him.

"It's such a historic building; it should be preserved," I said.

Around 30 students at the Tarmon National School in Castlerea listen to a presentation about my father' s life story. Jacinta is seated at the right

Chapter 7 -
The Bush Telegraph & the Rising

In 1916, my dad was eight years old. He and other students probably didn't learn about the building rebellion or the history behind it, at school.

"There would have been censorship. If there were any reports in the papers, you wouldn't get the truth," said Anthony Tuohy, the historian from Castlerea.

But, he added, there were other ways word spread.

"They had the bush telegraph," news carried from person to person, often when coming together around the hearth and at the local water well, like the one across from my grandma's cottage in Bookalagh.

The community well the Keanes, McNamaras and Devaneys shared

"You tell me, I will tell someone else and they went on to tell someone else that the rising was taking place," Anthony said.

And, he added there were the seanchaí, the storytellers, like Michael Tigue from Williamstown. The seanchaí told about Irish history in their ballads, songs and stories. They'd delve back into history to tell of the many rebellions before this one to put into context what was happening in current times.

Michael Tigue from Williamstown was one of the last traditional story tellers around Roscommon and Galway counties (From Anthony Tuohy's collection).

Michael most likely spoke about Oliver Cromwell's murderous campaign in the 1600s. Then, jumping ahead in time recounted how Padraig Pearse founded the St. Edna school to teach Irish youth their history and language and led the 1916 rising.

All of the children's eyes were on Michael as he read one of Pearse's writings, like the one he wrote in November, 1913.

"It is more than an historical great struggle that is going on in Ireland. It is a battle of two nations. We have to undo the English conquest of Ireland. We have to re-establish in Ireland her supremacy. So, the Irish movement in Ireland is not only a political movement. It is much bigger and much more complicated." [16.]

As the storyteller came around to speaking about the Irish rebels, Brian was there along with other youth from the area.

"Coming into town, I saw volunteers marching up the main street of Castlerea. It sounded like the determined rumbling of a spring storm," the seanchaí said speaking so softly the children had to lean forward to hear him.

"Here and there, I noticed a familiar face of one farmer or another who had joined the cause to rid Ireland of the English yoke. But, there were others who jeered and hissed, calling the rebels a menace, and why didn't they just let well enough things be"?

"The rebels are planning on taking over Dublin soon," the storyteller said, raising his voice for emphasis.

The rebellion took place on Easter Monday, April 24, 1916.

One of the brave men who stood by Pearse was James Connolly. He led the Headquarters Battalion of 220 volunteers from Liberty Hall to the General Post Office and commanded military operations there throughout the week.

Irish rebels taking over a building during the 1916 rising

During the course of the uprising, Connolly was shot and badly injured. He was subsequently arrested, convicted and sentenced to death for his part in the Rebellion. Despite only having days to live, he was executed at Kilmainham Gaol after dawn on May 12, 1916. Unable to stand because of injuries, he was tied to a chair and shot to death by a firing squad.

Connolly was one of 7 signatories of the Irish proclamation for freedom who were executed soon after the rebellion, along with nine other leaders without representation or trial.

Seven signatories of the Irish proclamation who were executed

Eamonn Ceannt, executed May 8, 1916

Thomas James Clarke, executed May 3, 1916

James Connolly, executed May 12, 1916

Sean MacDiarmada, executed May 12, 1916

Thomas MacDonagh, executed May 3, 1916

Patrick Pearse, executed May 3, 1916

Joseph Mary Plunkett, executed May 4, 1916

Other executed leaders

Roger Casement, executed August 3, 1916

Con Colbert, executed May 8, 1916

Edward Daly, executed May 4, 1916

Sean Heuston, executed May 8, 1916

Thomas Kent, executed May 9, 1916

John MacBride, executed May 5, 1916

Michael Mallin, executed May 8, 1916

Michael O'Hanrahan, executed May 4, 1916

William Pearse, executed May 4, 1916

In Ballymoe, families were especially attuned to what was happening because one of their own, Eamonn Ceannt, was executed.

According to a narrative about his life, Ceannt joined the central branch of the Gaelic League in 1899 where he met Pearse and Eoin MacNeil. These meetings engaged him in the Irish nationalist movement. In 1907, he joined Sinn Féin, then the Irish Republican Brotherhood, to fight for Irish independence.

John Brady noted in his book *Ballymoe* that the execution of Irish sons and daughters outraged the Irish people so much they threw their support to the cause of Irish independence supporting the Republican party, Sinn Féin, in the December 1918 United Kingdom general election.

Sinn Féin won defeating the Nationalist Irish Parliamentary Party, IPP.

In Brady's book, a poem by Lily O'Brennan honors Ceannt's life and his ultimate sacrifice to Ireland.

Eamonn Ceannt

He walked apart. God molded his childhood.

To understand His ways. Unobtrusive and quiet.

Nature appealed to him and the lark's lilt

Was ever in his heart and on his lips.

And when he grew to boyhood, she called him

And brought him to her fount and there he drank

A nation's purifying draught in History, Language and Song.

And when he grew to manhood's dreams

She placed a sword into his hands

And sent him forth to quell the foreigner

Who stole her mountain slopes and pasture fields.

And when he died, she clasped him to her breast

And coined and called him patriot.

But God who molded him a child

And made him in his fuller years

Great and kindly and good

Placed a crown upon his head

And called him martyr.

Chapter 8 -
War of Independence
1919-1921

In the aftermath of the elections, Sinn Féin's elected members refused to attend the British Parliament in Westminster (London), and instead on Jan. 21, 1919 formed a parliament in Dublin, the First Dáil Éireann ("Assembly of Ireland"), which declared Irish independence as a Republic.

The British pushed back outlawing the newly formed government sparking the War of Independence, also called the Black and Tan War, that raged on until 1921.According to Wikipedia, the conflict developed gradually in 1919 with the IRA confiscating weapons and freeing Republican prisoners, while the Dáil was building an independent state.

"In Dublin, they (the IRA) started to get organized in little bands around the county. They would raid; they would shoot at the British and RIC (Royal Irish Constabulary) barracks. They would intimidate their (enemies.) But they would never go face-to-face. They would hit and run and disappear. It was much like the Boer War. They were very poorly armed, just shotguns and revolvers. These were the IRA. That was the tactic; you rarely faced a regular army because you would lose. They were outnumbered, and the arms of the British and police were far superior," said Ganly.

A tour guide in Dublin further explained, "Since the time the British came to Ireland, it's been one big battlefield, more than 800 years at war. The Irish created guerrilla warfare, hit and run – used when you are fighting big armies and you don't have enough men – that's why you had the bombings, the snipers: it was the only way to fight them."

In 2016, Gillian Greene, a third-grade student at the Roxboro school in Mrs. Eithne Fallon's class, provided an account of one of those raids — the *Four Mile House Ambush.*[17] Gillian's detailed report includes maps, articles, newspaper accounts, graphics, diagrams and photos.

She wrote that it was the first major ambush carried out by Irish volunteers. The ambush encouraged other nationalists to carry on more attacks against British forces. Gillian states this had a ripple effect throughout Ireland boosting the War of Independence. The ambush, which occurred on October 12, 1920, resulted in the deaths and injuries of four RIC men and one Republican volunteer - John Conroy of Rathconnor who Gillian notes is buried in Ballinderry Cemetery.

The British responded to the Irish assaults by sending in the notorious Black and Tans, the band of mercenaries my dad often referred to.

"They were the scruff of England, and they were brought over to Ireland," said Micky Sheir from Ballymoe.

"Some would have been men who fought in the first world war who had seen all of the horrors of their comrades getting killed and wounded and they didn't give a damn about discipline. They were brought in to augment the regular (British) police force because a lot of their men were shot in the war. They didn't care about keeping the peace. If there was an outrage by the IRA or the Sinn Féin, they would gather up every young man, they didn't care who they were, they would beat them up and threaten to kill them, just to get information out of them. They were rough, very rough. They would rob and steal. In Knockcroghery village, a village in mid-Roscommon, they burnt it to the ground. All the factory was burned too," explained Jimmy Ganly.

Added Anthony Tuohy, "They were also here in Castlerea, the Tans. They did (horrible) things. They tied (resisters) on the back of cars and lories and dragged them down the road."

He remembered how his mom used to tell him how she feared them.

"In the middle of the night, my mother would get up to make a bottle for my eldest brother and there would be a knock on the door by a British soldier who was watching the house," he said. He wouldn't leave until he was satisfied that she was not sending out a coded message to the IRA.

"Everyone has a story about the ruthless brutality of the Black and Tans passed down to them from the parents and grandparents," said Jimmy Ganly.

Maureen Sullivan, who babysat my brothers and I in Detroit in the 1950s, shared one when my daughter and I visited her one summer.

"My mother, (Kitty Sullivan) would talk about Ireland. (Kitty and Tommy Sullivan were my mom and dad's best friends)," she recalled.

Maureen said the Black and Tans would walk in, take over." Chiming in, Maureen's daughter Kitty who heard stories growing up added, "My grandparents told how the Black and Tans put a burning cross on a family's lawn when they found out they were Irish Catholic."

Bloody Sunday brought world-wide attention to Ireland's War of Independence. On November 21, 1920, the day began with the IRA setting out to assassinate members of the Cairo Gang in Dublin, a group of British intelligence agents. The IRA killed 14 of the Cairo Gang and one member of the Black and Tans. [18.]

Retaliating later that day, the RIC and Black and Tans opened fire on a crowd at a Gaelic football match at Croke Park killing 14 members of the public, including a woman and a child, and injuring dozens more. In the evening, three imprisoned IRA members were tortured and killed at Dublin Castle after allegedly trying to escape.

Following Bloody Sunday, both sides engaged in killing sprees. More than 1,000 people were killed between January and July 1921, about 70% of deaths during the War of Independence.

A memorial near Jacinta's home honors James Mound, one of the volunteers fighting for a united Ireland. Around the same time, Jacinta would take me to see another memorial, which led to sharing my dad's story with the students at the Tarmon National School. [19.]

Cormac Beatty (Lf) and James Beatty (Rt) stand on either side of independent freedom fighter James Mound's memorial on April 6, 2021, the 100-year anniversary of his death

My dad was 11 years old when the War of Independence, *Cogadh na Saoirse*, began.

Like most Irish at the time, his family and neighbors supported an independent Ireland.

But their livelihood working on the farm had to be attended to. There was peat to cut, fields to plow, crops to harvest and animals to feed.

"It was hard work," my dad said.

In those days, peat was cut by a slane, a sharp, angled tool. After it was cut, it was wheeled to a dry place, then stacked it into a reek.

Good quality was called "stone turf."

But, whenever family members could take a break from their daily chores, townspeople and farmers helped the Republican cause making safe houses, leaving front doors open so resistance fighters could slip in and out of sight, providing them with food and clothing and giving words of warning.

Republicans looked down on those who didn't help.

In Anthony Tuohy's photo collection, there's a photo of several young people playing in Castlerea's Main Street courtyard. On the wall behind them is painted BOYCOTT MULARKYS in bold letters.

According to a source who didn't want to be identified, the owner, Mrs. Mularky, told the IRA soldiers and anyone who was curious that she was open for business and she didn't care where the business came from. To discourage folks from doing business with her, IRA foot soldiers walked up and down the footpath in front of her shop.

While some didn't trust her, my source said she saved many lives.

"Only for her, there would have been a lot of IRA fellows arrested and executed. (Overhearing talk in her shop or confidences shared with her), she would get word out to their mothers to get their sons away because there were warrants for their arrest. If it wasn't for the Mularkys there wouldn't have been an IRA man within 20 miles of Castlerea. They would have been lifted and probably executed," he confided.

In another black-and-white photo from the early 1920s, resistance to British occupation is depicted. Dozens of young Republicans are marching up Main Street. The inscription on the back identifies the men as Castlerea volunteers marching in opposition to Ulster volunteers.

Castlerea Republican volunteers marching to join the fight against Ulster (Loyalist) volunteers

I wondered if one of the young resisters might be my dad. My dad mentioned to my brother Brian and me that he'd been put in front of a firing squad during the conflict. Fortunately, he added with a smile, he got away when someone bribed the guard. My brother said he understood that was also part of the reason he went to America.

"I was told he was on the run from the British since he was associated with the IRA," Brian said.

"It didn't take much for the British to arrest someone, especially if they thought they were IRA sympathizers," said Jimmy Ganly.

Concurring Mickey Sheil of Ballymoe said, "I wouldn't be surprised. You had informers at that time, the same as you have them today."

Finbar pointed out, "You see there were four Keanes, James, John, Michael and Brian, and they were able-bodied men. (The IRA) probably wanted some of them to join them, you see. That was in 1921."

With growing support for the IRA from Irish citizens, the British government began to loosen its grip on Ireland for the first time in 800 years.

"When the Irish War of Independence ended, the mighty British Empire lost some of its power for the first time ever. We were on the way to independence at last!" wrote Gillian in her story of resistance.

Both sides agreed to a ceasefire. The post-ceasefire talks led to the signing of the Anglo-Irish Treaty, An Conradh Angla-Éireannach, on December 6, 1921.

Prime Minister David Lloyd George signed as a representative of the British government and Michael Collins and Arthur Griffith signed the Anglo-Irish Treaty on behalf of the Irish Republic.

Britain kept six counties in the north under its governance — Fermanagh, Antrim, Tyrone, Down, Armagh and Londonderry.

According to a review of historical figures by the BBC, De Valera, who was President at the time, didn't show up for the signing because the treaty partitioned the country and he fought for a united Ireland.

De Valera stepped down as President when the treaty passed and associated himself with the Fianna Fail party, which won elections in 1932. He was subsequently elected prime minister (Taoiseach) three times and then president of the Republic, a position he held until 1973. Under De Valera's rule, the cultural identity of the Irish Republic as Roman Catholic and Gaelic was asserted. De Valera died in August of 1975.

Chapter 9 -
The Civil War

The Anglo-Irish Treaty caused brothers, sisters, neighbors and friends to draw sides.

Civil war broke out on June 28, 1922 between the pro-treaty Provisional (Free State) Government and the anti-treaty IRA.

One of the first Irish casualties was Michael Collins himself who was shot and killed in an ambush by anti-treaty forces on August 22, 1922. He was known to have said after signing the treaty that he was also signing his own death certificate.

During the conflict, resistance fighters who wanted a united Ireland blew up bridges, cut down trees to block roads and stopped news from coming in so people had no idea what was going on.

In Castlerea, around 300 treaty resisters took over Clonalis House, the old O'Conor estate. On a tour of the historic dwelling one summer, the guide pointed to areas where bullets tore through the house. [20]

The Clonalis House in Castlerea is the ancestral home of the O'Conor Don, a direct descendant of the last High King of Ireland. Today, guests are welcome for tours, lodging and fine dining

As one story goes, when the Free State army, the ones who were pro-treaty, ended up hearing about the IRA's occupation, they sent a tank to Castlerea.

The IRA wouldn't come out, so the Free State army started shooting and barged through the heavy oak doors. Once inside, they arrested around 60 volunteers who fought against a partitioned Ireland. The rest made their escape through the back door.

On the most part there was little damage to the heralded house since someone from the estate reached out to both armies and asked them to stop shooting because the house was historically significant built in 1878.

Amongst the Clonalis House collections are 100,000 volumes of Irish documents dating back to the O'Conor Don family, direct descendants of Ruaidrí Ua Conchobair, the last High King of Ireland. The O'Conor Dons are the only Royal Gaelic family left in Ireland who are still living on part of their lands. I was proud to learn from Finbar my grandmother, Bridget Connor, was a descendant of this notable Irish dynasty.[21]

The civil war ended in May of 1923.

Anti-treaty forces — those who did not want a partitioned country — lost. Northern Ireland has continued to be under English rule since that time.

A year later my grandfather died. He was 68 at the time of his death on October 17, 1924. According to his death certificate, the cause is cited as "probably heart disease".

My grandmother was by his side.

My dad was 18 when his father died.

John, James, Michael, Celia and Delia, my dad and my grandma were still living at the cottage. It appears that Patrick passed away by this time, too. Patrick hasn't been forgotten though. My nephew is named after him.

After his dad died, my dad most likely went to London or Dublin to earn some money for his passage to America, which the family had decided was the best thing for him to do.

Leo Finnegan from the Williamstown Heritage Society said there were plenty of opportunities.

"Construction, road work or working on farms," he said.

There was also plenty of discrimination.

Public signs often read: "No Irish, no dogs" and "No Catholics or Irish need apply."

The same derogatory messages were directed towards Native Americans in the States.

To get to either London or Dublin, Brian walked or caught a ride to the Ballymoe station located a few miles from Bookalagh.

One day, Rita Morgan took me to the site where he would have caught the train.

"I used to pick up my sister here in the 1960s," Rita recalled.

Today, the deserted building emits an eerie feeling with many untold stories sealed within and draped over with lush, green foliage. Forgetting about the past, now the train zooms by the old station on its way to Castlerea to pick up riders around the area.

Rita Morgan points to the deserted station where
the train to Dublin used to stop near Ballymoe

On the taxi-cab tour around Dublin, my guide pointed out Turn-of-the-Century apartments on North King Street.

"While in Dublin your father would have lived in a one-bedroom called a bed-set, like this one. He shared the toilet and bath. It was about a pound a week (in your dad's time)," he said.

Chapter 10 –
The Leaving - 1930

When he was 22 in 1930, my father had saved enough money for passage to America and booked a ticket on the Ship Cedric out of Liverpool. The Cedric, operated by the British White Star Line, was a 20,000-ton ocean liner that crossed the Atlantic in four-and-a-half days.

Bernard 'Brian' Keane boarded the Cedric for America in 1930

He was the only boy in the family of eight to emigrate. I found his name on the passenger list with the help of a heritage specialist at Epic

Ireland's *Family Heritage Centre[22]* in Dublin. He was one of about two thousand passengers.

Spokesperson Fiona O'Mahony stands in front of a heritage poster inside the Irish Family History Centre in Dublin where visitors can search for kin

After I returned to the States, I had the opportunity to talk by phone to 91-year-old Padraig Beatty of Castlerea, Jacinta's uncle-in-law, who was born the same year my dad left for America.

Padraig Beatty riding a bicycle was a common form of transportation in Ireland during the 20th Century

Recalling what it was like growing up in the midlands of Ireland at the time, Padraig said the most memorable time of year was the Christmas Day dance in Ballymoe. People from surrounding towns like Castlerea and Williamstown traveled to Ballymoe for the annual event.

Jean Higgins from Williamstown described what local dances were like in a letter she wrote to me at Christmastime in 2020.

"All the ladies stood on one side of the hall and the men on the other, so the men walked across the floor to ask the ladies to dance. Those were good times," Jean recalled.

I remember going to a Christmas party with my mom and dad when I was a teenager and my dad said, "Let's have a dance." I was surprised that he was such a good dancer, patiently teaching me the steps, since I never saw him dance with my mom, who always said she had two left feet.

I imagined he learned to dance at the dance hall in Ballymoe.

Other than the dances, the farm work and a few shops, Padraig said there wasn't much going on. There were small farms, a fair once a month, the general store, a car dealer, a barber shop and a nail factory, he recalled.

Retired teacher Peggy Kennedy said the same thing when I visited her one day at her home in Ballymoe.

"Your dad, the reason he left, it wasn't for the promised land. There was nothing here; it was all taken from us. You couldn't own your own land, you couldn't get an education, the language was taken from you, everything was taken from you. You worked for pennies and buttons, just to survive, that's what your father (experienced)," she explained.

"He had no choice but to leave," said the Dublin tour guide.

Besides his mom and family, Brian would miss the rain, especially when it crashed down, hit the ground hard and bounced off again, like miniature, fun loving-jack rabbits.

It made him smile, like most things did. His mom always told him he was the most agreeable child of them all, always with a smile and funny saying to lighten things up.

One thing for sure, he thought he wouldn't be missing cutting peat – dig, cut, lift, stack; dig, cut, lift, stack; dig, cut. lift, stack — all day long.

But he would miss the Irish heather, moss and bog flowers. He'd made a point of learning about them – wild daisies. asphodel, sundew, bilberry and cranberry flowers to name some, along with the numerous species of birds — the stonechat, a delicate apricot-chested bird, the ever-watching kestrel ready to pounce on a small mammal and the meadow pipet that reminded him of a lark with a long tail.

The kestrel is often observed hovering above boglands searching for small mammals – Roscommon Heritage poster series

Rousing him out of his memories, "Here's to Brian!" Michael, his younger brother toasted as he tipped up the pint of ale in his hand.

"Yes, here's to Brian!" chimed in his brothers, sisters, aunts, uncles and several neighbors gathered together in the front room of my grandmother's cottage during his American Wake.

Raising her drink, his sister Celia scrambled up next to him and shouted, "May he have a safe crossing and may his new life in America bring him prosperity, for we have little of that here in this poor country."

Brian smiled, savored the toast, then slowly approached his mammy who was standing by the fireplace. It had been her lookout for the gang of kids she'd raised for the past several years alone since his dad had died.

She was dressed in her mourning clothes, a black shawl and black dress. As a keener, soon she would start wailing for the loss of her favorite son.

She looked down as Brian approached her. She knew it would be the last time she may ever see him. The last thing she wanted was for him to see her with tears in her eyes.

Brian knew she wasn't one for talking about emotions, so he kissed her on the cheek, and gave her the bouquet of wildflowers he had picked on the way back from the bog – wild daisies, bright coral poppies, delicate pink marsh peas and butterfly orchids.

Wild daises flourish on the green hills and valleys of the Irish countryside

She thanked him shyly and looked away.

He would miss his mom, even if she was always after him. She seemed to be harsher on him than the others. Looking over the crowd of folks at his American Wake — his mom, brothers John and Michael, and sisters Celia and Delia, the McNamaras and the Devaneys — Brian wished his dad was among them.

Breaking his train of thought, Celia reached for his hand and said, "Let's have a dance, Brian," and at that he twirled her around and the dancing started.

The night before, Brian had packed his suitcase with his belongings: a few shirts, a couple of pairs of pants and socks.

Now, the cardboard case sat by the door looking small, stark and lonely, much like he felt leaving them all behind.

But so, he must go. There wasn't much for him in Bookalagh and Ballymoe. John or James would get the farm. Michael was trained as a blacksmith, Celia and Delia were set in marriage. He said a silent prayer for his father and little Bridget and Patrick.

The next morning Brian picked up his suitcase and climbed on the buggy trap where his brother Michael was seated and waiting for him.

"I've got to be off now, Mammy," Brian called. She turned away and started walking down the path the opposite direction from where he was calling not wanting to watch as he walked away for the last time.

John called after Brian, "It's OK Brian, she doesn't mean nothing by it. We'd better be going."

Brian wanted to run after her, but if she rebuked him even more, his heart would break for sure.

As Michael readied the horse, Brian cried out to his mother, "Don't worry Mammy, I will be back one day."

Michael drove slowly as to have as much time as possible with his brother as he could before reaching the Ballymoe station for the train to Dublin.

At the station, they said goodbye, tears streaming down their faces. "I will write for sure," Brian said, "and I will be back. May God keep you all."

From Ballymoe he traveled to Dublin and then took a ferry to Liverpool where he boarded the ship Cedric to America.

The Crossing

On the dock, Brian looked out at the ship parked in the harbor. It was the largest ship he'd ever seen. He picked up his suitcase and fell into line. He could hardly breathe. He felt like a sardine in a slimy, stuffed can.

He was glad mammy had packed him some food; it was going to be a long wait. The sun beat down as the crew ushered passengers, mostly Irish, on to the decks. He wasn't sure where to go so he just kept quiet and followed along. Down the growing passenger line, he noticed a familiar face. It was his cousin, Kevin, whom he hadn't seen since they were in primary school. Kevin had grown into a strong, handsome man.

"Hiya! Brian!" Kevin shouted. "Fancy meeting you here," he said with a wink as he ran up to Brian and cut in line.

Brian was so happy to have family by him, especially after the heart-wrenching leaving and his mammy's cold response when he said good-bye. He knew she was still thinking it was the old days when family left and never came back. But he knew times had changed.

These were his people, his family, his neighbors, his dog; of course, he would return after he had made his way in the world.

He missed his dog. He'd renamed her from Meadow to Rebel before he left.

But now he had to leave that behind. He had his future to look forward to in America where anything was possible.

"How do you come to be on this same ship, Kevin?" Brian asked.

"Well, you know how it is; not much for me on the farm. Dead end for sure, you know and to hell if I will go to England and work for the Brits. Best to do something else with my life, eh?"

At that, a loud horn blew and a booming voice called out for those who had general fares "Make yor way down to the bottom quarters. Bunks are first come first served, so better be quick!"

Passengers scrambled to get their suitcases and a few fights broke out. In the chaos, Brian lost track of Kevin. Almost losing hope he'd find him again, he felt a hand on his shoulder and there he was, steering him down a hidden staircase and opening a door to a good-sized storage area.

"Our accommodations," Kevin said, adding "You really don't want to sleep in the quarters, they're full of bugs. If you catch something, they'll send you back."

"Looks good," Brian said, happy to have Kevin by his side.

"Here," Kevin said, "Something to take the edge off," handing him a flask full of good Irish whiskey.

Brian accepted with a smile.

"What are you going to do when we land?" Brian asked as he spread out his jacket on the floor and put an extra sweater on.

"I have no idea. I just left, didn't wait around for a wake. Said goodbye to my mammy, shook da's hand and walked away. They watched me go with not a word."

That may have been the easier way, thought Brian remembering all the tears and his mammy's cold shoulder.

Changing the subject, Kevin said, "I hear it's not a cakewalk over there in America, either, especially after the stock market crashed. A lot of people on this boat are going to have a mighty hard time. There are no jobs, lots of people out of work. I'm sure there will be plenty of signs, 'No dogs, no Irish here.'"

But, Kevin added, "If anyone can handle it, we Irish can. We've been through it all – starvation, colonization, Brits, bullets and beatings, taking our language away."

"Let's drink to that!"

"Here's to a new life in America!" Brian toasted feeling more assured about his future than he had been.

Chapter 11 -
The Great Depression

The Statue of Liberty rose out of the harbor like an ancient Irish mythological goddess.

Leaning over the rail of the ship's top deck, Brian called out to Kevin.

"Isn't she grand?" Brian yelled as Kevin rambled up next to him, wrapping a tattered blanket around his shoulders with one hand and covering a cough with the other. They stood silent and transfixed as the Cedric slowly maneuvered through the harbor past America's historic symbol of freedom and welcome to immigrants and refugees from around the world.

Holding a torch in her uplifted arm and a tablet with the date the United States declared independence, Lady Liberty stands over 300 feet tall from the ground to the tip of the torch. She was a gift from the people of France to the people of the United States dedicated on October 28, 1886.

French sculptor Frédéric Auguste Bartholdi designed her and as a finishing touch coated her with copper. Over the years her shiny bronze coloring turned a hazy shade of green from exposure to air and the water.

This seemed fitting to Kevin, who felt it was a special welcome to the Irish.

"I can tell she loves the Irish," Kevin said with a wink.

Looking up, Brian recited what he had learned about the statue back in Ireland.

"The broken chains near the feet of the monument symbolize that the struggle for freedom ended in complete victory and the end of tyranny.

"The seven spikes of the crown are rays of light representing the seven seas and seven continents of the world.

"The torch represents the values of liberty and enlightenment and the rays indicate the spread of these values."

"That all sounds good to me," Kevin said, coughing a little more.

Getting concerned about his congestion, Brian pulled out a bottle from his pocket.

"Here, Kevin, take this. It's medicine that my mom makes." he said.

As the Cedric entered the New York harbor, a ship's official yelled for people to get their belongings.

Brian reached out to Kevin.

"God be with you, Kevin."

"And to you, Brian," Kevin replied.

Then, people started pushing them forward and Brian came face to face with a gruff guard calling for his passport.

As the guard scrutinized his documents, Brian looked around to see what line Kevin was in and was shocked to see him being led away by two officials. After getting his passport back and a nod to board the ship, he pushed through the crowd until he was face to face with another guard, this one holding a stick over his head.

"Can't you read? You can't go that way! One more step and I'll give it to you," he said.

Stepping back to the authorized line, he asked a man standing next to him, "What will happen to him?"

"He probably didn't pass the health exam. He'll be on the next ship back to Ireland. Nothing you could do, unless you want to go back with him," he said.

"No matter how much I miss home, I can't go back," Brian thought and said a prayer that Kevin would recover and they would meet again.

As soon as Brian stepped off the ship leading to the streets of New York city, he realized Kevin had been right about the hard times in America; it was desperate times — the peak of the Great Depression.

With his suitcase in-hand, he walked by people lined up for food rations, others for jobs, many begging for help with their hands stretched out while others jeered, "Go back where you came from."

He wondered why his sister hadn't mentioned anything about the American hard times.

The welcome he felt from Lady Liberty quickly diffused into the blackening night. Cars and trucks flooded the streets. They honked when Brian didn't get across by the time the light changed. On the sidewalk he was pushed aside as he looked for a place to stay. His efforts to find lodging were met with slammed doors and posted signs "No dogs and no Irish here."

Feeling helpless and lost he looked out at the street and wondered which way to go. He had to find a place to sleep and a way to call his sister. Sleeping on the street was out of the question. Folks back home would be shocked.

Brian had ten U.S. dollars in his pocket. His sister Mary had sent the American currency to him so he could get lodging until he found a job and saved enough for a train ticket to Detroit where she lived.

He stopped in front of a bed and breakfast that seemed warm and inviting. Looking more closely, he noticed a symbol of a four-leaf corner in the bottom window pane, a message to Irish immigrants that they were welcome.

Before ringing the bell, he breathed a sigh of relief, put a hand through his thick, dark hair to smooth it out, buttoned up the top of his dress shirt and put on the tie his mother had given him.

"This was your father's" she said to him. With his hair combed, suit-coat, white buttoned-up shirt and tie, he looked handsome and stylish.

"There will be help along the way," he remembered his Aunt Honor telling him during his American Wake.

The door opened and he was warmly greeted.

"A thousand welcomes to you!"

The next few months flew by after getting a job on the docks loading and unloading cargo. To him, it was an easy job. He'd had plenty of experience working on the docks in England and loading and unloading turf in Bookalagh bog fields.

By Christmas, he had enough money for a ticket to Detroit.

It wouldn't be Ireland, which had the brightest and happiest Christmases anywhere, he thought, but at least he would be with his oldest sister and her family.

He hadn't seen Mary, who had left Ireland when she was around 20, for many years.

As soon as he could, he would get a job and apply for citizenship. He didn't want to be a burden to them. They had enough on their hands, raising a family and trying to get by when there was little money or jobs to be had.

Mary had given him directions to the house from the bus stop. Instead of using his money, he decided to walk, something he was used to in Ireland.

He passed through the city centre where there were as many cars and trucks as there were in New York City.

But people here were nicer than those in New York City. They tipped their hat to him, smiled and a gentleman even waited while he crossed the street instead of honking.

His sister's directions led him to a tree-lined street with white framed houses each with a porch and a swing. By the time he found Mary's house it was getting dark and many of the houses had Christmas lights on. His sister's house shone the brightest.

"I will leave the light on for you," she had said.

He put down his suitcase and rang the doorbell.

The door flew open.

"Brian, you are home, come in, come in!" Upon entering, a new family surrounded him, his sister, her husband Fred, his niece Mary Ellen and nephew Freddie.

"You're welcome a million times over," they repeated.

There was lots of field work available around Michigan and Brian found a job right away picking fruits and vegetables.

Laughing to himself, he thought cutting peat was good experience for that, and thanked his lucky stars again he had that to claim, while lots of the other young men looking for work were city lads and the only fields they'd ever seen were ones requiring a bat and ball rather than a shovel and a hoe.

Coming home to his sister's house at night he felt good putting a fistful of dollars in her cookie jar knowing later on she would reach for them, grab her coat and head to the corner store to get milk for the children.

Besides needing to save money to get his own place, he needed to get US citizenship, so at night he went to the local community center to study for the test. He already knew quite a lot about America. His mother, always encouraged him to read. The library in Castlerea was one of his favorite getaways. In the last couple of years, he'd taken out every book on the United States. He memorized presidents, national holidays, the capitals of each state and the Pledge of Allegiance.

At night in Detroit, he'd meet up with his Irish friends and they would take turns having him answer questions they knew to be on the test, because they had taken it themselves.

Five years after he'd arrived in the United States, he became an American citizen. But getting a job was nearly impossible. It was 1935 and the country was still in the midst of the Great Depression.

Drought was also turning the nation's heartland into a dustbowl uprooting thousands of farmers. Some 15 million Americans, one of every four workers, had lost their job. Across America, they stood in line for hours hoping to find work.

I remember visiting my Aunt Mary at her house in Detroit when I was a child. One time, we sat in the living room and another time in the kitchen. She had white hair, wore an apron and served us tea and cookies. Usually, my mom would do all the talking on when we visited folks, but this time she didn't, she sat back and let my dad and his sister quietly talk between themselves. I was too young to have any idea what they were talking about. But surely, they talked about the time when he first stayed with her during the Great Depression.

After immigrating to the US around 1920, Aunt Mary settled in Detroit, married and raised a family

After we left, there wasn't a word said about the visit. I don't remember ever getting any cards or letters from Aunt Mary or any word from any of our other relatives. There seemed to be an unspoken understanding not to talk about Dad's past, so we never brought it up and he didn't either.

Chapter 12 -
Civilian Conservation Corps

After my mom passed away in 2003, I found photos of my dad in Idaho dated in the 1930s. I'd never seen these photos, either.

In one, he glances up as he walks towards the camera on a barren piece of land. The other side of the photo reads "Twin Falls, Idaho". Twin Falls was one of the largest Civilian Conservation Corps, CCC, sites in the country.

In a second, he's walking near a dam; while in a third, he's sitting on the steps of a bridge made out of logs smoking a cigarette; in a fourth, he leans against a fence, a lake and a hill in the background. A 3-by-2-inch photo made in an instant photo booth shows him posing with a dark-haired man. His friend is wearing an open high-collared shirt, while my dad is slightly more dressed up wearing a white shirt and a tie with polka dots and a cowboy hat. His sense of humor and quick wit come out in the writing on the back of the photo: "Public enemy No. 1 — $500 dollars reward last seen in Twin Falls, Idaho."

Barney Keane in Idaho during the height of the Civilian Conservation Corps

In each photo, he has the look of a person who has accomplished something and is looking forward to the future.

This is how I unravel what happened. By this time, he was going by Bernard, shortened to the nickname Barney instead of Brian.

Always on the lookout for opportunities to help out his American family, Barney learned about a program called the Civilian Conservation Corps established by President Franklin D. Roosevelt as one way to put Americans back to work while improving natural resources and building community structures.

Speaking about the Depression-era works program, Roosevelt said in one of his famous quotes, "In creating the Civilian Conservation Corps we are killing two birds with one stone. We are clearly enhancing the value of our natural resources and at the same time, we are relieving an appreciable amount of actual distress and conserving not only our natural resources but also our human resources."

To Barney it sounded like the perfect opportunity, except the program was for 18-to-25-year-old young men. He had turned 27 in 1935.

But luck was on his side. The program was so successful in alleviating unemployment and providing support to families, the U.S. Congress approved the Emergency Relief Appropriation Act of 1935 on April 8, which included upping the qualifying age to 28.

At the Civilian Conservation Corps offices in downtown Detroit, he filed in behind a line of young men about his age.

When it came to his turn, an official with a CCC badge on his shirt barked at him,

"Your identification!"

Pulling his newly issued citizenship card out of his pocket, he laid it on the counter.

Taking a good slow look at it, the gruff official said, "Here are your induction papers. You are now in the CCC, Roosevelt's tree army. You will need to get to Twin Falls, Idaho by a week from today. It's up to you how you get there," he said louder than needed.

From studying for his citizenship test, he knew Idaho was out west somewhere. How he was going to get there was another problem.

Walking back to his sister's house, he thought about the many ways he had left Ireland — first the train, then walking, on a borrowed bike, then the boat across the Irish sea and the Ship Cedric to America.

He would get there.

After saying a tearful goodbye to his sister and the family, he headed for the train track with only the clothes on his back and a paper bag full of sandwiches Mary made for him.

The train track loomed in front of him. It was dangerous. Hitchhikers were called scabs. They were beaten if run down, kicked off and left for dead. But it was the only way to get there on time. He checked the schedule at the train station and walked along the tracks to see what doors were left open at night.

"Be careful. Don't take your shoes off in case you have to run, and keep everything close by you," advised one of the veteran train riders when Barney asked for advice.

It would take three days to get there. He was told it was best to change trains often and always at night.

The land grew flatter and browner as the last train he hopped neared Twin Falls, Idaho. There were no sheep or cows or horses, no rolling green hills, no sign of any rain for days to come. The flatness sprawled out in all directions, just scruffs of foliage on the prairie and a pond here and there. A knot built up in his stomach.

Finally, a sign said 'Camp Minidoka, Twin Falls, Idaho.'

Barney fit right in.

He was used to hard work. He was glad he had worked in the bog cutting peat and on the docks in England. He would put his skills to work for America and his life ahead.

Barney Keane in Idaho in the 1930s

In 2018, I traveled to Boise, Idaho to research Idaho's Civilian Conservation Corps history and visit Twin Falls. I spent hours in the local library's *Idaho & Pacific Northwest History Collection* poring through archives. [23]

This band dugout in Twin Falls, Idaho is one of the many public works projects constructed by the Idaho Civilian Conservation Corps in the 1930s

The "tree soldiers" were required to serve for six months, then could re-up for up to two years. They worked 40 hours a week earning a dollar a day, or $30 a month. They were required to send most of the pay back home to help support their families. It was enough to put food on the table. At the time, sandwich ham was 16 cents a pound, sausage 25 cents, rib steak 21 cents and coffee 15 cents.

In addition to the monthly check, CCC members received free lodging, three square meals and education and training.

Most of the recruits who arrived in the camps were underweight and some even malnourished.

"A lot of the boys came in pretty hungry, pretty thin, and the first month, six weeks, they'd gain 10 or 11 pounds," said one of the cooks in an account of the CCC.

Enrollees wore surplus one-size-fits-all army uniforms.

When they issued the clothing, they didn't bother asking the size. "If you complained, they'd say don't worry about it, you will grow into it," one CCC member recalled.

Rusty Clemons, host of a Veterans' broadcast, described his findings about camp operations: "Things were strict. You had to polish your shoes, keep your uniforms pressed, keep your bed made. When the (officials) came in and flipped a quarter on your bed and it didn't bounce, they'd tear it up and you'd make it over again. It was good training."

In the field, the CCC members worked for the Forest Service, Park Service, and Bureau of Reclamation, but back in camp they were under the Army.

In Idaho, among their many tasks, crews constructed elaborate rock picnic shelters at different parks. About the service, CCC staffer Fred Blood said, "The boys collected all this rock and jack hammered and brought it by truck for the masonry man. You can see where they've used the chisel and the hammer to chip it out so that it'd take the bump off and kind of square it up so it would fit in place. The old-time hand masonry people knew how to do it and did a heck of a good job."

Two of the slogans the young men repeated daily were, "You can't keep a good man down," and "Try, try again." Growing up, I often heard my dad saying the same phrases.

Roosevelt's tree army ran from April, 1933 to June, 1942 when the US engaged in WWII.

Bruce Reichert, host of *Outdoor Idaho*, said the conservation corps had a major effect on Idaho and the rest of the nation. Roosevelt's tree army planted millions of trees, built thousands of miles of roads and trails, stocked fish, constructed campgrounds, band stages, lookouts, bridges and picnic areas and reconstructed historic sites. They also drained swamps, constructed diversion dams, laid telephone lines, fought forest fires and pests.

Four federal departments, Labor, Agriculture, Interior and Army established the CCC camps. Total men enrolled: 3,463,765. Average number of camps operating in one year: 1,643.

The program benefited millions of families.

Referencing the success of the historic effort, during the coronavirus pandemic, U.S. President Joe Biden proposed a similar national works project. The Los Angeles Times called it a modern version of the Depression-era Civilian Conservation Corps. Biden's CCC – the Climate Conservation Corps - proposes to use government programs to provide jobs and training for public projects aimed at preparing for, mitigating or forestalling some of the worst environmental impacts of global warming.

Mom

Born in 1910, my mom, Jovita, was called Jo Keane when I was growing up. She was originally from Minnesota, a granddaughter of German immigrants. When she was about 16, her dad moved his growing family to land in the badlands of Montana where he set out to farm and ranch. It was not an easy life. The summers brought drought and grasshopper infestations; in winter, snowstorms cut off food and water to cattle.

Like my dad, my mom didn't like farm life. Around the same time, he was taking a ship across the Atlantic, she was finishing high school and had her sights on moving to Chicago to follow her dream of becoming a nurse, which she did. She was certified by the state of Illinois as a registered nurse on July 6, 1938.

To pay for her training, she worked as a maid for some very rich folks. Telling me about it, she said it didn't turn out so well. Although she seldom drank, she said she lost the job because she opened up the liquor cabinet one night and tried out different brandies and liquors.

I would never have suspected she ever bent the rules. Raising us kids, she was strict, never tolerating rudeness or bad behavior of any kind, always on us to do chores, homework and get good grades. I remember her saying quite often, "Everything in moderation is a good rule to live by."

Both my mom and dad impressed on us the importance of higher education, which we all went on to accomplish.

I found more evidence of my mom's lighter side in photos dated from 1936 to 1940 of her and fellow nurses on holiday making snowballs during a winter snowfall and posing like Hollywood movie stars on top of a tour bus. They are having the times of their lives laughing and joking around in front of the camera. She might have been on a break before starting her first nursing job in 1938 at Grace Hospital in Detroit.

My dad had headed back to Detroit from his stint in the CCC in late 1936 or mid-1937.

My mom in Chicago in the 1930's

My mom on the left with her friends on a break from nurses' training

My Mom

Back to the Midwest

My mom told me she met my dad through mutual friends, Bud and Gin Malone. Gin had bright red hair and a pixie smile. I remember her because my mom said at cocktail hour, her drink of choice was gin and tonic.

My mom and dad hit if off right away. And soon they were a couple hanging out with my dad's Irish community - best friends Tommy Sullivan from Mayo and his wife Kitty from Cork, Bud and Gin Malone, George and Helen Murray, Patrick O'Leary and his sister Annie O'Leary, Margaret and Fred Donahue and many others. They often went to the Tiger baseball stadium together, rooting for the Michigan team and out at night to the local pub, the *Hole in the Wall*. I remember going to games when I was a kid intrigued by the crowds and watching out for the man who called out, "Hot dogs here!" Best hotdogs in the world at Tiger stadium.

Tiger Stadium - historicdetroit.org

Between building structures and roads for the CCC, working on the shipping docks and railways in Dublin and England, and back on the farm in Ireland, my dad had gained loads of experience. And he had a good old-fashioned work ethic – you do the job and you do it right until it gets done.

"He would have picked up skills. The fact that he worked on a farm, he'd be used to turning his hand to any job, building of stone walls, making hay, cutting turf, and he would be strong as well. He wouldn't be afraid of hard work or he wouldn't be afraid of working long hours or working in bad weather. These things were parcel of life. Hard work wouldn't faze him at all," responded Jimmy Ganly when I mentioned my dad's work achievements.

After his stint in the CCC, he got work at Continental Motors. I recently found this out through his Army discharge papers. But, growing up, I always thought he worked at the Ford Motor Company, since we always had a Ford.

With a steady job, my dad came round to asking my mom to marry him. But there was a snag. As the story goes, one night he got wrapped up in a card game and the only valuable item on him was her engagement ring, which he lost. He never said how he got the money together to buy another ring.

Besides this mishap, my mother's father didn't like him. My maternal grandpa was a stern old man.

He didn't like that my dad was known to have a drink or two and that he smoked.

But my mom told him he was a decent man, with a lot of friends, good values — a good Catholic who wanted to have a family like she did.

Next to all the others she had met, "He was a great guy," she said. "The best!"

They were married on Nov. 21, 1940.

By that time, my dad had been in the States for ten years. My mom was 30 years old and he 32. I found a photo of my mom in a trendy hat, a long coat with a fur collar, nylons, laced-up high-heeled shoes, gloves, standing next to a friend just as stylish. I imagine it's her wedding day.

My mom on the right, possibly her wedding day, with a friend

Years later, my grandpa had a change of heart about my dad. I remember during a visit, my mom retold the story of their initial animosity, then turned and nodded, and said, "Now look at them. They're the best of friends."

It was hard not to like my dad with his gentle, non-assuming manner, warm smile and quick wit. And he was always willing to lend a hand. To my mom's displeasure, I remember how he always pulled over and gave the nod for one hitchhiker after another to share a ride in our Ford.

Chapter 13 –
WW II

Their future — everyone's future — was uncertain. The world was at war.

By 1940, Adolf Hitler's Nazi regime and the Axis forces, intent on taking control of the world, had invaded Denmark, Norway, Netherlands, Belgium, Luxembourg, France, Poland, Czechoslovakia, Austria, British Channel Islands, Italy, the Soviet Union and France. [24.]

According to [25]*Facing History*, by the summer of 1941, British intelligence agents learned about "systematic mass murders in Lithuania, Latvia, and later Ukraine." In a BBC broadcast on August 14, 1941, British Prime Minister Winston Churchill spoke to the world of the atrocities.

"As [Hitler's] armies advance, whole districts are being exterminated. Scores of thousands, literally scores of thousands of executions in cold blood are being perpetrated by the German police troops upon the Russian patriots who defend their native soil ... And this is but the beginning. Famine and pestilence have yet to follow in the bloody ruts of Hitler's tanks. We are in the presence of a crime without a name." [25.]

American journalists on their return to the U.S. in 1942 reported hundreds of thousands of Jewish people in Latvia, Estonia and Lithuania had been killed by Hitler's "new order."

Joseph Grigg of the UP reported: "One of the biggest slaughters occurred in Latvia in the summer of 1941 when 56,000 men, women and children were killed by S.S. troops and Latvian irregulars." [25.]

Beginning in September 1941, every person designated as Jewish in German-held territory was marked with a yellow star. Tens of thousands were soon being deported to the Polish ghettoes and German-occupied cities in the USSR. [26.]

Like their neighbors and friends, Barney and Jo listened to President Franklin Roosevelt's fireside chats to keep informed on what was going on in Europe.

On December 29, 1940, just a month after they were married, Roosevelt made a "call to arm and support" the Allied powers, which included Britain and France, with weapons, planes, trucks and tanks.

In his broadcast Roosevelt impressed on Americans that a German victory in Britain would greatly compromise the safety of the United States, emphasizing that aiding Britain would save Americans from the agony and horrors of war on American soil.

In his speech, he appealed to Americans to stand up as the "arsenal of democracy" as though it was their own country at war. He called on the nation to unite with swift cooperation in producing vast shipments of weaponry to aid Europe.

At the epicenter of auto manufacturing, Detroit answered the call immediately giving workers new designs to duplicate as it transitioned from autos to the production of weapons and vehicles of war: jeeps, M-5 tanks, and B-24 bombers to fight Hitler's horrifying regime. The factories cranked out one bomber an hour. I imagined my dad hard at work.

As motors whirred behind him, Barney ignored the rising heat of the factory. He picked up the intricate part and looked it over, set it down and picked it up again. The weight wasn't quite right so he pushed it against the bench grinder harder until the sides fit perfectly in the machine part he was building. After he built the part, he double-checked their standards and every time they were right on mark. He smiled to himself. It reminded him of how his father taught him to be exact in cutting and stacking peat in the old country. Each piece was a work of art, his father would say as he showed Brian how to cut, bind and stack it. His neighbors always noted the Keanes' handywork.

Wikipedia reports that with a workforce of over 36,000, Briggs built aircraft gun-turrets, doors, wing components, bomb doors, heavy and medium tank hulls, trucks and ambulance bodies, B-29 Superfortress and the KC-97 Stratofreighter tanker aircraft. [27]

The Continental Motors factory produced aircraft parts, combat vehicle motors, along with engines for R-975s and tanks. The company ramped up production for "vital war materials" as the heat of WWII raged on. By the end of 1943, the company's East Jefferson plant employed 8,000 hardworking Detroiters, most of whom worked eight hours a day, seven days a week.

At the Ford Motor Company's Willow Run plant an assembly line one-mile-long produced B-24 Liberator bombers. By the end of the war, Ford built 86,865 complete aircraft, 57,851 airplane engines, 4,291 military gliders, and thousands of engine superchargers and generators. In addition to aircraft, Ford plants built 277,896 of the versatile vehicles (tanks, armored cars, and jeeps). [28.]

Barney was happy to be able to contribute his part and take care of his family too. He knew well what it was like to be occupied and dominated by a colonizing government.

Roosevelt honored Detroit's contribution by declaring it "The great arsenal of democracy."

On December 7, 1941, the Imperial Japanese Navy, one of the Axis partners, ambushed the American military base in Pearl Harbor triggering the U.S. to enter the war.

The call for service was everywhere. On radio, television and city streets, messages beckoned young men from 18 to 45 to register for the draft.

In 1941, my parents' first child, whom they named John after my dad's youngest brother, didn't survive. My mom and dad were devastated.

Their hopes for another child were realized when my brother Brian was born in April of 1943.

They were delighted with Brian's birth but the future was uncertain as Hitler's demonic power spread like cancer in Europe, Africa and the Pacific.

62 Figure
My dad holds Brian during a trip to Montana just months before he left to serve in WWII

63 Figure
His shoulder patch showed he was initially assigned to the 97th Infantry Division, the Triden

64 Figure
The Trident

My dad was 35 when he joined the Army.

Brian was 8 months old in December of 1943. My mom and Brian carried on, as other families did, in a two-story walk up on Springle Avenue.

Before he left, there were many get-togethers with their Irish community in Detroit. In one photo, my dad is dressed in an Army-issued uniform and Brian is on his lap. It may have been just days before he left for the service.

Brian sits on Dad's lap during a going away party in 1943

My mom is sitting in front of him and around them are several members of the Kopp family, close family friends. The women have bouffant hairdos swept back off their faces, curls trailing down their shoulders and dressed in their Sunday best.

My mom told me she understood what it was like to be a single parent, because she was one for three years during the war. All that time, food and other necessities were rationed. I understood an inkling more of what this was like when the coronavirus hit in 2020 and people started hoarding supplies, leaving store shelves empty.

During the war, with meat going to the troops, Spam, the processed canned meat, became a popular item. My mother continued to use it long after the war. I remember many Spam sandwiches and Spam and eggs.

My dad talked less about what happened during WWII than he did about growing up in Ireland, so I had very little to go on when I started looking into this era of his life.

There was one time he opened up about it when I asked about the Purple Heart tucked away in a top dresser drawer.

For injury during combat, Barney (Bernard P.) Keane received the Purple Heart

We were in the basement sitting at the bar.

He pulled up his left pant leg and showed me scars from shrapnel that hit him during combat somewhere near the French/German border.

He said, while he survived, a young German soldier didn't.

"He died in my arms," he said with a shattered look as if it had just happened yesterday. Throughout the war, Hitler recruited children as young as 8 years old. [29]

My father looked so distraught; I didn't press on.

He turned and poured himself another shot and never spoke about it again.

After we talked, every so often I would go back into my mom's and dad's room to look at his Purple Heart. As I got older, I realized what a large weight my dad carried all this time. Not only the loss of his family in Ireland, but the trauma from events that occurred during the war.

Looking back at photos, I noticed the Trident patch, representing the 97th Army infantry division, on his military shirt in the picture my mom gave me. According to Wikipedia, in December 1943, the 97th trained at Camp Swift, Texas, then moved to Fort Leonard Wood, Missouri in February of 1944.

In a group shot of the Replacement Training Center – RTC 54B — about 60 soldiers, each holding a rifle, stare into the camera. My dad is sitting in the front row, far right. In faded letters below is written "A Training Battalion, March 11, 1944," which placed him at Fort Leonard Wood, Missouri. He never mentioned he'd been in Missouri. [30.]

At this time, he most likely was still in the 97th infantry division.

Barney Keane's training group, March 11, 1944. Barney is in the first row, last soldier on the right

Operation Nordwind – [31, 32, 33, 34, 35]

The 97th infantry division was headed to the Pacific Theatre after training at Leonard Wood, Missouri; but in a turnaround moment 5,000 troops were sent to the European front to push against Hitler's last-ditch counter-offensives building up at the French/German Border in the Alsace-Lorraine region, according to a Wikipedia reference.

Author Flint Whitlock state that there were two, The Battle of the Bulge and Operation Nordwind.

After about a year of training in the states, my dad arrived in Europe October of 1944. Sometime afterwards, he was transferred from the 97th to the 7th army's 45th infantry division, Company A, 157th, the Thunderbirds. The Thunderbirds had begun their push to the French/German border in the fall of '44 after claiming victories in Sicily, Naples and Rome. It was the same time Barney had arrived in Europe.

The 45th infantry was originally a National Guard unit drawn from Colorado, Arizona, Oklahoma, and New Mexico and made up mostly of Native Americans. The Thunderbird is a Native American symbol representing power and strength. Each of the four sides of the patch represents one of those four southwestern states. The color red symbolizes bravery and valor, yellow is a symbol of warmth or energy, according to the Oklahoma History Center Education Department.

I thought it coincidental that my dad and I both had close ties to Native American tribes. I worked for tribal governments and Indian organizations for many years and he fought beside Native Americans during the war.

I imagine he might have known several Navajo Code Talkers, who used their indigenous language as a code that couldn't be broken, helping win the war. I was honored to have interviewed Thomas H. Begay, one of the last remaining code talkers, several times for the *Navajo Times*.

On the tail of the Battle of the Bulge, Operation Nordwind started the 1st of January, 1945. They fought in the frozen woods of Vosges east of Epinal, France, taking over Alsace saving the Moder River line and then Reipertswiller, one of the most famous battles. They fought in freezing weather while faced with barrages of shelling, mortar fire and tank assaults by Hitler's forces who were more than ever, with the war finally ending, determined to push the Americans back.

The counter offensives were unexpected moves, according to Flint Whitlock who writes for warfarehistorynetwork.com. Many thought by the end of 1944, the war was nearly over, he noted.

"Germany is beaten, the optimists opined. She's on her last legs, others said. Her defeat is inevitable, and sooner rather than later. Such an outcome certainly seemed within the realm of possibility. Tens of thousands of Wehrmacht and SS troops in France were either dead or in POW camps. Paris and Brussels had fallen to the Allies, and one city, town, and hamlet after another had been liberated," Whitlock notes in *Operation Nordwind: The Other Battle of the Bulge*.

But Hitler wasn't backing down.

"To protect his southern flank once Wacht-am-Rhein (the Battle of the Bulge) was launched, Hitler had devised a secondary counteroffensive - "Unternehmen Nordwind" (Operation North Wind)—this one directed at stopping the 6th and 7th Armies and French regiments," writes Flint Whitlock in warfarehistorynetwork.com.

In the middle of January, the 45th U.S. Infantry Division was just south of the village of Reipertswiller when it was attacked by the 6th SS Mountain Division with rockets, mortars and artillery. Offwiller where my dad was shot is about 5 miles from Reipertswiller. My dad was admitted to the hospital on January 22, 1945.

The 57th regiment ended up losing 158 men killed, 426 captured, and some 600 wounded or evacuated due to illness or injury, including my dad.

With US troops getting reinforcements from the French First Army in the Colmar Pocket, by January 25, the German counteroffensive ran out of steam, with the Americans controlling all of Alsace-Lorraine except for a strip of the northeastern corner of France from Lauterbourg to Gambsheim, according to Whitlock.

"In the end, the Germans, hobbled by their unwieldy command structure, had no reserves left with which to follow up on their gains, and the stubborn Americans—the cold, hungry, battered, and bandaged Americans—refused to be defeated," Whitlock said summing up Hitler's very last offensive.

The distinctive yellow on red Thunderbird insignia of the 45th Infantry Division stood out in the badges and medals my dad received for his combat service during WWII

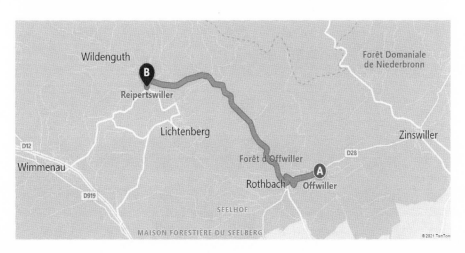

Offwiller where my dad was shot is 5 miles from one of the most recorded battles during Operation Nordwind

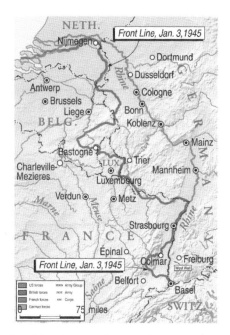

The red line shows Strasbourg on the German/French front line January 3, 1945 – Flint Whitlock

The blue line shows the distance between Strasbourg and Offwiller where my dad was shot near the German/French front line. It's about 35 miles from Strasbourg to Offwiller

Barney Keane in uniform during WWII

Here's how I imagine it unfolded.

Shells fell around Barney. The decimating blasts nearly broke his ear-drums. With dirt and smoke all around him, he could hardly make out the enemy with swastikas on their helmets. Nevertheless, as trained, he and other 157th, A company Thunderbirds focused their weapons strategically, hitting as many as they could. Retaliating, a shell blew up close to Barney. He'd been hit. Blood gushed out of his leg reddening the ground around him. He wrapped his leg with a torn-off section of clothing.

Hearing what sounded like the painful call of a child, he quickly finished the makeshift bandage. Struggling, he crawled through the foliage towards the cries. He thought, maybe it was a child from the village who got caught in the crossfire. But it wasn't. It was a German soldier not even 11 years old. "How can that beast Hitler send children to be killed? What kind of atrocity was this man?" thought Barney.

The boy looked at him with pleading, piercing blue eyes. "Ich will meine Mutter!" (I want my mother), he cried.

Barney cradled him in his arms. The boy calmed down. His blond hair fell in curls out of his helmet, now askew.

As the child gave his last breath, Barney heard a loud American voice call out, "Hey, there's one of ours over here. He's alive!" Barney watched as his bandage oozed blood, then everything went black.

He woke up three days later. When the French-speaking nurse came by, he asked where he was. But she couldn't understand him, so she put up her hand indicating, "Wait a minute."

Then, in a flash of an eye, a big redheaded man stood in the doorway with a huge smile on his face.

"Somehow, Brian, we tend to end up in the same place," said Kevin, still using Barney's boyhood name.

Barney sat up, forgetting his injured leg.

"Kevin, it's you! My God! It's so good to see you! Come here, come closer!"

With difficulty Kevin slowly edged towards the bed.

"Not exactly in one piece, but very much alive," he said.

He stepped slowly on one foot, crutches holding up his weight.

"Oh Kevin! This is too much, way too much," Barney cried.

"It's not OK," Kevin said, "but I'll be all right. So many blokes are plain out dead. I'm not dead." He pulled a flask of Jameson's from his hospital garb and offered Barney a swig.

Catching up, Kevin told Barney he eventually cleared immigration after the medicine his mom had given him clicked in and his cough went away. He settled in New York City and when the US entered the war, he was one of the first to enlist.

"Where are we, anyhow?" asked Barney.

"At the 11th Evac hospital in France," Kevin answered.

According to medical records, Barney was hit by shrapnel in late January, 1945 in Offwiller, France. Offwiller is 30-minute drive from the front line at Strasbourg.

After being shot, my dad was transported to the U.S. 11th Evacuation Hospital.

The WWII U.S. Medical Research Centre 11th field hospital unit history[36], notes that all units of the 11th field hospital were shifted from Southern to Northern Alsace in January of 1945, in the vicinity of the 7th army which was engaged in stopping German troops crossing the Rhine River near Strasbourg.

After being shot, my dad was transported to the U.S. 11th Evacuation Hospital

Outside view of the 11th Evacuation Hospital in France

On January 7, 1945, hospital headquarters moved by truck from Sainte-Marie-aux-Mines to Sarrebourg, a distance of 59 miles. On January 13, 1945, headquarters moved seventeen miles forward to Saverne, a more centralized location. [37.]

This medical note documents that Barney was hospitalized January, 1945 at Offwiller France for injury "incurred when shell struck."

The blue line shows the location of the 11th Evacuation hospital in Saverne, France to where Barney Keane was shot near Offwiller

Around 80,000 U.S troops, including the Thunderbirds, pushed back the German infantry and Hitler's very last offensive on the French/German border. During the conflict, the 157th Regiment suffered 158 men killed, 426 captured, and 600 wounded or evacuated, including my dad.

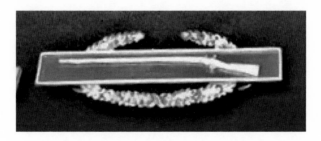

The badge my dad received recognized his sharpshooting skill

Along with the patches for the 97th Infantry Division, 45th Infantry Division and the Purple Heart, my dad received a Rifle Sharpshooter qualification badge, the Army Air Corps 9th Air Force Class A patch (signal corps) and a US Combat Infantryman badge (CIB).

The CIB is awarded to infantrymen and Special Forces soldiers who fought in active ground combat. It recognizes the inherent sacrifices of all infantrymen, and that they face a greater risk of being wounded or killed in action than any other military occupational specialties.

On his discharge papers my brother Brian passed along to me, he also received an EAME Theatre ribbon with three bronze stars, a distinguished unit badge and the WWII Victory medal. He is credited for "assisting and capturing and holding enemy positions and destroying enemy personnel; familiar with scouting, map reading and small arms repair and maintenance serving in the European theatre of operations for 15 months."

After the war ended, he proudly wore the *Ruptured Duck* badge. Depicting an eagle inside a wreath, it was issued to service men and women about to leave the military with an honorable discharge. Some thought the original patch looked more like a duck and because it meant soldiers were going home, the popular saying was, "They took off like a *Ruptured Duck*," hence the nickname.[38.]

Growing up, we never had guns in the house and he never spoke of any ability to shoot them. But, certainly coming from a farm in Ireland, he would have grown up hunting to help feed the family.

Amongst my mom's belongings I found a silk purse embroidered with "My Dear Wife" on one side and "U.S. Army" and its insignia on the other side.

Finbar recalled, "I remember him saying, showing me the pictures of the wife and his son, that he looked many times at Jovita's and Brian's dear faces, and said, 'I may never see you again.'"

Based on medical records, my dad was discharged from the 11th Evacuation Hospital on January 22, 1945. The war raged on.

He went on to serve in the 45th until the end of the war, according to his discharge papers from the U.S. Army. In April of 1945, the 45th and two other US military units liberated the Dachau concentration camp. "They found thousands of mostly emaciated prisoners. The U.S. soldiers also discovered several dozen train cars loaded with corpses" – history.com.

At some point, between the time he got out of the hospital and the end of the war, he was given a lateral assignment. A swirling LA was penned on his hospital discharge.

In looking back at the return address on copies of letters from my dad to my Uncle Michael (my cousin Sheila sent them to me) during the war or soon after it ended, read the 438th Signal Heavy Construction Battalion, known as the Signal Corps, troops who installed and repaired communication lines. I learned the 438th was part of the 9th Army. A 9th Army patch is among the insignia in his war memorabilia.

One letter was dated August 24, 1945, from what looked like "Viernheim, Germany," and another September 15, 1945, from Nurenberg, Germany.

Along with other major events he participated in, he never mentioned the extraordinary and critical role the signal corps played during WWII.

The Signal Corps installed telephone lines, dug holes, climbed and planted poles, placed wire and repaired breaks close to active combat. (online image)

"They operated so close to the front that signal corpsmen often were atop poles stringing wire as infantrymen plodded through the hedgerows," stated the booklet [39.] *Lone Sentry —Service: Story of the Signal Corps," published by the Stars & Stripes in Paris in 1944-1945.*

They worked in minefields, under constant enemy mortar fire, supplying most of the wire communications for France, Belgium, and into

Germany. Hundreds of miles of new cable were installed, telephone lines laid, switchboards connected and channels opened. [40.]

My father and thousands of other Irish-Americans bravely defended the country that had greeted them with signs hung on shop door posts, "Dogs and Irish not welcome here." Native American WWII war veterans, like decorated US Army scout (103 Infantry Division) Joseph Medicine Crow from the Crow Nation, said they were faced with the same hateful, derogatory message when they returned home.

His honorable discharge from the 45th Infantry Division was on January 9th 1946.

Chapter 14 -
Post war

My dad's neighbor, Finbar McNamara, was about 11 years old when my dad came back to visit his family in Ireland after the war. He was 38. He felt lucky to be alive and leave the sound of bombs blowing up, the sight of swastikas, the immense power of panzers, freezing nights and days, the killing of his fellow soldiers and his own near shave with death behind.

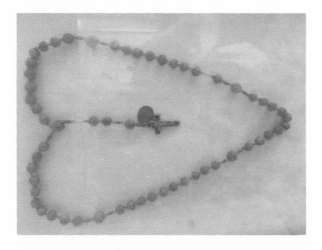

A soldier gave this rosary to my dad who gave it to his mom after the war. As a family heirloom it was given to my brother Brian. It now hangs framed in Brian's and Mary's home in Florida.

But, even after the sounds of battle fade away, war lingers.

At the time, what we call post-traumatic stress syndrome today, it was known as "shell shock" then and dismissed as unimportant. Without evaluation or treatment, an incident just weeks after being in combat on the frontline, was bound to happen.

On my trips to Ireland, I heard different versions of what took place during my dad's visit when a car backfired or a kid with a toy gun let out a loud "crack". The way-too-familiar noise triggered flashbacks of the front line.

It seemed like for some, excluding Finbar and my cousin Noel, it was the only memory of my dad that survived over the years. I thought this isn't only how he should be remembered, which has also been a motivation in writing his story.

He, like other WWII soldiers, and those who came before them, suffering from PTSD, dealt with the terrifying nightmares and flashbacks on their own. PTSD wasn't diagnosed until after the Vietnam war in the 1970s. Still today many veterans go undiagnosed and untreated.

Back to the States

When he returned home to Detroit, three years had passed. The family settled into a white-framed house at 4411 Ashland with a fenced-in back yard in a quiet, tree-lined Detroit neighborhood.

"I didn't know who he was, since he left shortly after I was born. That's my earliest memory," my brother Brian said.

Barney getting to know his son Brian after being away for three years

Growing up, Brian remembers Dad as soft-spoken, reserved and a good provider, who only missed work once in his lifetime when he was injured in a motorcycle accident.

"He was out of work for several months. I remember him limping around with his leg in a cast. That is the only time I remember him taking off work," he said.

Even then, he made sure the bills were paid and food was on the table by working on cars in the garage.

Some of Brian's fondest memories of our dad are when he hit baseballs to him, sang old Irish songs with our sister-in-law Peggy's dad, (Jerry's wife) Jim Ray, listened to the radio when the Detroit Tigers were playing baseball and helped him with a variety of projects.

But like with me, he didn't speak to Brian much about the past.

"He never spoke to me about his time in the service, or what happened to him in combat," Brian recalled.

Back in Detroit, like other veterans, our dad moved on with his life returning to work at Continental Aviation. But he didn't stop serving the country. He signed up for Reserve Duty in the Signal Corps, a duty he took on until 1949.

My mom went back to work at a Detroit hospital.

They were happy days again connecting with the Irish community.

Many of the group were members of the Gaelic League.

"My mom, Kitty (Sullivan), was queen one year," our babysitter Maureen said proudly.

Kitty and Tommy Sullivan

"They had house parties a lot. Your dad and my dad (Tommy Sullivan) played cards. I think they played poker and euchre," she said.

While my dad worked as a machinist, Tommy Sullivan worked at U.S. Rubber. On weekends, Maureen said they helped each other out with projects around their houses. During the war when my dad was away, the families shared whatever they could — ration stamps, canned foods, milk, and bread.

After the war, Kitty got sick. Maureen said my mom was there constantly to take care of her.

"Jo was fantastic," Maureen said.

My brother Jerry was born in Detroit in 1947 and I was born in '49. With my mom not taking off much time from work, Maureen became our regular babysitter; she even went out to Montana with the family during the summers.

"I really enjoyed you guys," Maureen said.

Brian (standing), Jerry and Colleen

"But Jerry was always getting into some kind of trouble," she added.

Giving an example, she told how Jerry, probably seven or eight at the time, took a part a radio and couldn't or wouldn't put it back together again.

"I was really upset with him. I was 13. It was all the entertainment we had at the time," she said.

Maureen told him, "You're really in trouble, Jerry!"

But, when Barney walked in, all he said was, "Hmm, the little man had a busy day."

"Barney was very easygoing, nothing upset him," she said.

Usually on Saturday nights, my mom and dad went out and Maureen came to babysit.

But Christmas was different. We always got to go Christmas parties. I especially remember one at Auntie Annie's.

Auntie Annie was an auntie to all the Irish children in the Detroit community

It's still as clear as day how I wandered around her huge three-story home in a Detroit neighborhood exploring upstairs and downstairs while the adults ate, drank and talked in the kitchen and living room. I thought it was the most remarkable house with a seemingly unending staircase for a little person with whom the adults had no bother. I remember the many stairs it took to get up to the second floor to peek into Auntie Annie's room shrouded with heavy curtains, piles of blankets on the bed, and lamps that cast a dim light on photographs of her Irish relatives. She may have immigrated to America around the time my Aunt Mary did.

In the 1950s, my family moved to Toledo, Ohio when my dad got a job at the Continental Aviation factory there. One of my earliest memories was leaving Poochy behind. I cried for days. My mom didn't want a dog in her new house. I remember she had trained him to stay out of the kitchen. He never stepped a foot in there. [41.]

In Toledo, my mom went to work at St. Vincent's Medical Center.

My brothers and I went to a Catholic grade school, not far from our house.

I remember trying to keep up with my brother Brian who walked me home from school.

When I was in high school, we moved into a three-story house with a basement and a sprawling back yard. It was quite a leap from the humble cottage in Bookalagh. My dad must have wanted to share this news and other news with his family back in Ireland.

The new house was the result of my dad's and mom's hard work. I don't remember my dad ever taking a sick day either.

My mom drove him to Continental Aviation before dropping me off at Central Catholic and starting her shift at St. Vincent's. He wore one of the shirts I'd ironed for him the day before and carried a metal lunch box with bologna sandwiches, cookies and an apple in it.

I never saw inside the factory where my dad worked. I only could imagine a long assembly line and my dad walking up and down supervising the production.

Once he said, "I get plenty of exercise. I walk miles a day."

He would come home with his shirts sweat-stained, but never complained.

During the Vietnam war, Brian was in the Reserved Officer Training Corps, ROTC, as a college student. After graduation, he entered the US Army Corps of Engineers in September, 1966. His assignment – Thailand. Before he left, my dad gave him a tour of the factory.

"I remember he asked me to come to Continental Aviation when I came home from Ft. Belvoir, before I went to Thailand. He was disappointed that I didn't have my uniform with me at that time. However, I got to see where he worked," he recalled.

"He became a master machinist," Brian noted.

"These skills would include lathe machining, blueprint reading, milling, numerical control, grinding, micrometer applications and supervision of others," he explained.

My dad's army discharge papers also acknowledged his machining expertise from his work at Detroit's Continental Motors from 1936 to 1943:

"Operated engine and turret lathes, planers, shapers and drill presses. Used micrometers, calipers and gauges. Reads blueprints, worked on steel and aluminum. Knows metal properties, tolerance of 1/2 thousands. Machined tank motor parts."

"I think dad was very proud of his trade, but became frustrated with others who were not nearly as skilled. He was a very smart (self-taught) guy, who worked with very tight tolerances on jet engines. I still have a micrometer that was his, along with numerous other tools," Brian added.

He was an inspiration to Brian.

"I had an interest in things mechanical, which I am sure I got from him. I would help him with body work on cars. I always enjoyed those times," Brian recalled.

Brian became a civil engineer and built a successful company in Florida.

After school, since my mom worked all day, I made dinner. Ham and potatoes, chicken and potatoes, meatloaf and potatoes. There were always potatoes, either mashed, baked or French fries. Maureen remembered every dinner was served with a potato of some sort in her family, too.

When TV dinners were invented. I didn't have to cook as much. I thought it the best invention of all as we ate and watched our favorite shows on TV. During the 60s, news reports were broadcast on the Troubles in Northern Ireland. My dad stared at the screen with a far-off look on his face.

"The Troubles will never be over. Catholics and Protestants will never get along," my dad said, and that would be the end of the conversation. Hearing this, it made sense that he couldn't stand our next-door neighbor, a Protestant whom my dad referred to on occasion as a "Goddamn loyalist".

Periodically, he would use more derogatory terms about Black and Tans, never explaining who exactly they were.

I wish I would have pressed on and asked him to talk about it.

I left home in 1971 to go to college at Ohio State, got married, moved to Arizona, got divorced, moved to California, then moved back to New Mexico.

I must have some traveler blood in me.

During that time, I earned my bachelor's degree at Ohio State and was working on my master's in journalism at the University of Southern California. In the midst of my studies, my dad suffered a stroke. My mom, also getting up there in age, couldn't take care of him and admitted him to the Old Soldier and Sailor Home in Sandusky, Ohio, also known as the Ohio Veterans home.

The Irishman aged as everyone does and smoking two packs of ciga-rettes a day, **along with his habit of drinking his fair share of spirits, caught up to him. My mom, not being able to care for him, placed him in a nursing home. Perhaps it reminded him of living under British tyranny, or the Nazis during the war. He screamed at the nurses and pull out his tubes.**

On calmer days, he dozed and dreamed of days gone by, himself the young man brimming with excitement, boarding the ship Cedric, the newly inducted American citizen headed west to help rejuvenate the country with new roads and bridges, the soldier fighting against tyranny, **the dedicated husband and father, the friend raising a toast to the "old country".**

My brothers and I visited my dad when he was in hospital and at the Old Soldier and Sailor Home in Sandusky, Ohio. Brian came from Florida, I came in from Los Angeles, and Jerry from Southern California.

I can't write about seeing him these last times without feeling the immense regret and sadness of not being there with him more. If there is any message to be carried away with this story it is this: Spend time with your parents before it's too late.

There at the home, if you can call the sterile surroundings such a thing, he sat slumped to the side in a wheelchair. A white hospital garment hung loosely around him. He shied his eyes away as if embarrassed. He didn't try to talk.

I held his hand as I sat next to him and told him about my studies and how I was getting on. He looked straight ahead without any sign that he understood or was listening.

"I don't know if he recognized me," my brother Brian said.

I think he recognized both of us.

But he was too sad and lonely to show it.

Chapter 15 –
Retracing my dad's footsteps

The red light on the answering machine blinked as I walked into my one-room apartment in Los Angeles. Pushing the button, I heard my mother say the three words you never want to hear: "Your father died."

I recall sitting down on my well-worn couch that took up most of the room in my small apartment.

I didn't feel alone. I sensed my dad's presence.

He sat in the only extra chair and took in the surroundings. His eyes settled on the photo of himself looking debonair leaning against a 1930s black Ford on a Detroit Street where he had first settled after immigrating to America, and another where he was dressed smartly in his Army uniform during WWII.

It seemed like I heard him say, "Those were the days. I was so full of myself."

He wasn't in pain or sadness anymore; he was at peace more or less, but I could tell something was missing.

While he came back to say goodbye to me, he didn't have enough time to say goodbye to his family in Ireland.

I wished he could stay longer and we could go together.

But before the wish was fully made, I glanced back over and the chair was empty.

I could hear my mom's voice instead of his.

"You should have gone back to Ireland with him," she scolded.

Now, all of that was too late.

"You really disappointed him," her voice railed in my head.

Catholic guilt poured out as fast as I could pour a glass of wine.

"I should have figured it all out," I thought.

Like my grandma made sure my dad had a good sending off in Ireland, my mom made sure he had a good sending off in Toledo. She was on the phone for days and nights calling friends, co-workers, neighbors and all the Irish families in Detroit. On the day of his funeral, they packed the church and the hall saying prayers and tipping their glasses to say goodbye to the Irishman who had been a friend to them. They knew him for his easy manner, kindness and generosity.

It was an outstanding sending off.

But my mom's words still haunted me.

I should have gone back to Ireland with him.

He would have been able to see his family again and I would have met my relatives.

In 2003, my cousin Mary Mulheir organized a Keane reunion at the White House in Ballyhaunis.

My cousin Mary (Celia's daughter) showing me a legendary Hawthorne bush

It was a memorable, yet surreal experience meeting relatives for first time when I was in my mid-50s — Mary, Aiden, Georgette, Bobby, Anne and Arthur Russell, Nora, Jimmy and Maureen. Most traveled from places around the world — Australia, England, Romania and my brothers Brian and Jerry and my nieces and nephews, along with Joanna and me from the U.S. From Dublin, Galway and Ballymoe, my Aunt Mary, my cousins Sheila, Basil and Mary Spellman.

I wished my dad could have been there.

For me, it was the beginning of filling in the blanks of my Irish history.

My cousins Mary Spellman (Delia's daughter) and Jimmy Cryan (Celia's son)

But I wouldn't return for another eleven years when I took on the task of writing my dad's story. That's when I met my cousin, Noel, who couldn't make it to the reunion.

On a trip to Kylemore Abbey on Ireland's west coast with my cousin Noel

From Castlerea, I took a taxi to Ballymoe where the driver left me off in front of St. Croan's Catholic church. As I wandered into the church, a lady who was working there asked me my business and I said I was looking for my cousin's house. "That would be easy to find, it's the house on the corner down the lane."

After a knock or two, Noel answered the door and I introduced myself.

"I'm your cousin Colleen from the states."

He didn't seem surprised at all. Long-lost cousins are always showing up in Ireland. But it's more considerate to call ahead.

Tracing Irish history

As a journalist, I'm inclined to follow up on leads, and my dad left a couple. What came to mind was his disdain for "loyalists" and the "Black and Tans." Besides my dad's curt mention of them, I'd only heard about either group in novels.

To fully understand the history, I traveled to Belfast in 2014 and 2015. Before going, I pitched stories to Steve Young, the publisher of *New Media Street Press*, an online alternative news and opinion journal. He gave me the go-ahead. *After the Guns Have Been Laid Down* published in 2014 and *Where the Rubber Misses the Road* in 2015. [42.]

For the stories, I covered the Orange Order parades on July 12th in Belfast, an event that has historically sparked resentments between Catholics and Protestants. Covering the parades helped me understand Ireland's history.

Orange Order members march through Belfast city centre on July 12th 2015

The 12th celebrations were first held in Ulster in the 18th Century. They celebrated the victory of Protestant King William of Orange over Catholic King James II at the Battle of the Boyne in 1690. William's win heralded the Protestant Ascendancy in Ireland.

If James had won, there would have been a different historical timeline. It was widely thought that under James, a Catholic king, discrimination against Catholics would end. During his short tenure as King, James had introduced laws for religious tolerance. However, the British parliament feared the he was trying to make England an officially Catholic country again. In the meantime, James' daughter, Mary, married William of Orange, making him heir to the throne. With that, the British parliament threw their support to Protestant William. William and Mary became King and Queen in 1689, a mark in time known as the Glorious Revolution.

But James, who had fled to France, wasn't giving up so easy; he regrouped. In March 1689, he landed on the shores of Dublin to fight for his throne.

In July of 1690, the two armies fought it out at the River Boyne. William won and James fled to France again. The Battle of the Boyne has become a memorable event in Irish history due to its symbolic Catholic/Protestant confrontation. [43.]

Messages I've read in travel guides dissuade visitors from going to Belfast during the 12th holiday for fear they might get caught up in the conflict. But, if you do visit during this time, you will most likely see the reality of the continued tensions, visible by blatant bashing of Catholics, the insistence on traumatizing Catholic communities and silent acts of resistance — many Catholics close up shop and leave town.

In 2014, on the night before the 12th parade, I took a taxi drive through the Protestant community where youth piled wooden pallets onto a pyre they were building for a bonfire later that night. It was huge! It must have been 100 feet tall. The bonfires are symbolic of the Battle of the Boyne, because King William's supporters built them to help guide him onto to the Irish shore.

Ken, the taxi cab driver, appeared nervous as we drove around the field. Several young men turned from what they were doing to watch us drive by.

"I don't want you to get out, just take photos through the window. They might start throwing stones," he said. Later that night, I took another taxi drive to a local park. As the clock struck midnight, hundreds of people had gathered for a bonfire – one of many around the city – as a loudspeaker played a catchy American-style country music tune about King "Billy" (William), and the announcer proclaimed the greatness of Britain.

All the while, the Irish Republic flag, with its tri-colors visible from a distance, flew tenuously on top of the pyre. Its fate sealed as a match was lit and a huge burst of flames brightened the night sky.

In local news that night, more provocative actions against Catholics were reported. A statue of the Virgin Mary was crushed at a Catholic church; an elementary student appeared with face paint on her forehead reading KAT (Kill a 'Taig – a Catholic), and like the Irish flag, Sinn Féin (Irish Republican) leader Gerry Adams' photo went up in flames.

"There's still hatred and mistrust here. Believe me, Colleen, get it into your head, these people still don't like each other," Ken, the taxi driver, said.

On the morning of the 12th, thousands of Union Jacks blew in the wind, on flagpoles in front of homes and businesses and strung across busy streets.

Orange outfits flooded the streets while marchers waved the red, white and blue Union Jack and displayed huge banners plastered with the face of William of Orange.

Paradegoers, many with British flags wrapped around their shoulders or their waists, waved more British flags as the bands passed by.

Marchers during the 12th parade, 2015 – Belfast

While Protestants reveled in the day's events, the marching reminded the Catholic population of the Troubles and hundreds of years of oppression, bloodshed and cruelty.

In the late afternoon, the loyalist bands made their way towards Ardoyne, one of the Belfast Catholic communities most traumatized during the Troubles.

"They (loyalists) should remember that people who consider themselves Irish would resent that (British) flag being flown in their face," explained Ray Mullan, the communications director for the Northern Ireland Community Relations Council.[44.]

"The flag issue is an example of that conflict that you will see around Northern Ireland around this time of year. People walking around see on the street the man who killed their father who is not in jail; people who have lost limbs and people whose health has been shattered because of assassination attempts or bomb explosions," added Mullan.

In 2015, marchers were determined to go down Woodvale Road and pass by the Ardoyne shops even though the Parade Commission, operating under a Northern Ireland law, restricted 12th marchers from walking through Ardoyne at the end of the day. It did however allow the marchers to walk past the Ardoyne shops in the morning. The conflict is presented satirically on You Tube[45]

As the parade marched on, I walked from the town's centre to the intersection where the marchers were headed. Rounding the corner of Ardoyne Road, I went up a slight incline near the roundabout to find Woodvale Road. In the distance I heard the boom, boom, boom of the drums, a monotonous humdrum that reverberated throughout the city announcing the marchers were coming this way.

Soon after I arrived around 4 o'clock that afternoon, Belfast police driving Land Rovers and dressed in protective gear drove up and methodically began putting together a metal-link barrier across Woodvale Road. Woodvale borders the Protestant community and leads into Catholic Ardoyne.

Parade goers are stopped by a police barricade during the 2015 July 12ᵗʰ parade

Standing behind Land Rovers, Belfast police brace for the onslaught of marchers determined to walk through the Catholic Ardoyne community

Journalists from Belfast, me from the United States, others from several countries stayed out of the way as they finished working and then parked their Land Rovers side-by-side across the road.

Just as they completed the barrier, the sound of marching feet, drumbeats and flute whistles grew louder. Soon a mass of loyalist banner-and-flag-carriers butted up against the barrier. Teens climbed onto the rock wall on the side of the street.

Angry that they couldn't get through, marchers called out profanities to the police and the small group of journalists. Then, amid the sound of obscenities and insults, glass bottles crashed down on us followed by a flurry of nuts and bolts, full soda cans, a ladder, a car's side mirror.

The pelting continued for more than an hour.

Belfast reporters donned helmets. Without one, I watched to see where the hurling debris was coming from so I could get out of the way.

Then, conflict broke out down the road in front of the Catholic shops.

By the end of the day, several Belfast police officers and journalists were injured along with a young girl run over by a loyalist, according to the nightly news.

That morning, a local man who just wanted to go by his first name, Gerard, and several other members of the Ardoyne community held up banners reading "Resolution is possible."

"Tensions could be resolved. All they have to do is go another way. Then, everybody is happy. But they just want to walk past our district and antagonize people," he said. [46]

During the 12th parade, members of the Catholic Ardoyne community call for a peaceful solution

Catholic Ardoyne, bordered on the west by a majority Protestant population, was one of the hardest hit Catholic neighborhoods during the 30-year civil war that left thousands dead and many more severely injured on both sides of the economic-political conflict identified by religious affiliation.

In 1998, both sides agreed to lay down their arms and signed the Good Friday Agreement, but Mullan says until the tension is resolved between Catholics and Protestants, there's not true peace.

"A new future is needed that is different from the past with no vendettas and no revenge," Gerard added.

Ray Mullan, Northern Ireland Community Relations Council

Cory and Cathleen (*Their names have been changed*)

The day before the parade, I visited Belfast's Lenandoon-Suffolk community. There, I learned firsthand what living amidst the tensions was like during the Troubles and how residents deal with tensions that percolate to the top during the marching season.

The Lenandoon-Suffolk community was fraught with violence on both sides of the conflict during the Troubles.

At a small strip of businesses sporting a fabric shop and a café on Stewartstown Road, I stopped to look at a memorial reflecting peace between the two communities.

Peace advocate Suzanne Lavery demonstrates how Suffolk and Lenandoon came together to put their handprints on a statue that reflects good will between Protestant and Catholic communities.

As I snapped some shots of the structure, a black sedan pulled up and a tinted window rolled down. "How ya doing, there?" came the question.

Thinking a complaint was coming about my photo taking, I told the driver I was a journalist working on a story about efforts toward peace and reconciliation.

Instead of admonishing me, which I expected, the driver said "We can tell you about that. Please, get in."

Sitting in the backseat of the dark sedan, I listened as Cory and his wife Cathleen (who didn't want their real names used) shared their history of the Troubles that was fueled by inequities and injustices towards the minority Catholic population that had continued since the penal times.

"My father being Catholic couldn't get a job because they were only for Protestants. Protestants had cards that gave them access to jobs — like on the Shipyard, there wasn't a Catholic that worked there. Those cards were passed down from generation to generation," Cory said.

Cory had a youthfulness about him even though grey streaked his dark, curly hair. I imagined him as a teenager all full of himself and ready to take on the world.

But, when he was growing up, Belfast was a battlefield and any efforts to reach his youthful dreams were stopped before they even started. He was thrown in jail in the heat of the Troubles without legal counsel or a trial when he was 16.

"In 1972, I was arrested. They put me in the Crumlin Road jail. I was the youngest political prisoner in the jail; (I) was terrified. At that age the only thing you are interested in is girls. I was in the wrong place at the wrong time," he said.

Cathleen, his wife of more than 40 years, was also picked up. Flecks of grey trickled through her hair. Back in the 60s, her bright blonde locks pulled back into a ponytail must have caught the eye of every guy on the block.

She told how she and a friend who also had blonde hair were arrested because someone had said two Scottish soldiers had been shot dead by two blondes.

"They (the Ulster police) literally tortured us," she said.

The Troubles started in 1968 and escalated after a street march in Derry by Catholics who banded together to protest unfair housing and employment opportunities, lack of voting rights, lack of representation in Parliament and not being able to buy farming land. [47.]

"This is what is going on around here," stressed Cory. "They (loyalists) want to stay in the majority, and they want to show they have the power. It's like tension 24 hours a day; it's like a bomb ready to explode. It's like Israel and the Gaza Strip, that is what I would classify it as. They have the upper hand."

But he added, not for long.

"(Protestants) are scared of the Catholic population. They know the Catholics are going to be majority here (eventually)," he said.

And now, Catholics were getting the better education and the better jobs.

"Even now, if you're in a bad area and a Protestant stops you and you don't respond, you could get one through the head," he went on.

It could be about something as trivial as a person's name or where they went to school.

"They don't like the name Mary, because Our Lady was Mary. Or they might ask about your loyalty to the Queen. People are afraid to open their mouth, you know. Sometimes you wonder how you survive from day to day. It's intimidating," he stressed.

Giving an example, he said it's difficult for his son to see his girlfriend who lives in the Protestant community of Shankill.

"Do away with flags and marching, you would do away with trouble. People could live together. If you keep on with it like this, there will be more trouble," he warned.

Opening up his newspaper, Corey pointed to a picture of a youth hanging up a poster that read, "Kill all Taigs," referring to Catholics.

"The biggest problem is the flags and the bonfires on both sides. There will never be any (peace) as long as there are flags and bonfires," Cory said, concurring with my dad's similar opinion.

Cathleen chimed in, "My mama used to say, 'There will never be peace daughter, in my day, but there might be peace in your day.' We are both 60; I can't see it in our day. I'm hoping for my kids' sake and my grandkids' sake … that it will come someday."

Falls Road

While I was in Belfast, I often walked up to Falls Road in west Belfast where 'peace walls' still separate Protestant and Catholic communities and murals depict memorable scenes from the Troubles. A mural of Bobby Sands on the side wall of Sinn Féin's offices at the corner of Sevastopol Street stood out for me.

Bobby Sands, a member of the IRA, died in prison after leading a hunger strike against British occupation of Northern Ireland during the Troubles.

This mural in Belfast honors Bobby Sands who fought for the rights of imprisoned Republicans during the Troubles

"I was only a working-class boy from a Nationalist ghetto. But it is repression that creates the revolutionary spirit of freedom," Sands is quoted in an online profile.

In prison, Sands pushed for reforms for incarcerated Irish fighting against colonial rule: identification as prisoners of war rather than as criminals; allowing Irish freedom fighters to wear their own clothes, receive visits and mail. Sands started his hunger strike in 1981 along with nine other Republican prisoners in the H Block section of Maze prison. He died from malnutrition on May 5, 1981. He was 27 years old and had refused to eat for 66 days. Nine other IRA supporters died on a hunger strike. Eventually, the British government gave proper political recognition to the prisoners, many of them earning their release under the 1998 Good Friday agreement. Sands final days were depicted in the 2008 Steve McQueen film *Hunger*.

Farther down the road on the corner of Northumberland Street is the Solidarity Wall depicting numerous images of international freedom fighters.

The Falls Road derives its name from the Irish *túath na bhFál*, an Irish petty kingdom whose name means "territory of the enclosures". [48.]

On a walk to the Republican district, I stopped in a shop just getting set up for the upcoming commemoration of the 100th anniversary of the 1916 Rebellion. John, the shop owner, pulled out stacks of boxes upon boxes just unloaded from a truck.

He told me to go next door to the pub and ask for Patrick. He could tell me about the Troubles, he said.

Patrick was easy to find. It was around noon and he was pretty much the only person in the darkened pub. He was in his late 60s and had been interned during the Troubles. Bent over and sullen, he looked like he had weathered more than one storm. He ordered a lemonade for me.

He was a man of few words, but those words were clear and to the point.

Being Irish, he said, discrimination was part of life.

"Back then, you couldn't get a house and if they asked you what school you went to and you say St. Thomas or any other Catholic school, you wouldn't get the job."

But today he said that loyalists aren't getting away with as much discrimination as they used to. Still, he added "In ways today, it's still the same."

Back at the souvenir shop, John unpacked Irish flags, figurines depicting the Irish rebel leaders: Padraig Pearse, John Connolly, Eamonn

Ceannt, Tom Clarke, Joseph Plunkett. T-shirts, shot glasses, mugs and tweed caps with Celtic designs spilled out of unpacked boxes.

John agreed that discrimination was still part of the fabric of the North's society, but there was a shift taking place.

"Now, Catholics have educated themselves and are getting most of the top jobs." He said time was a factor, too.

"Thirty years from now, I see a united Ireland, because we are going to be in the majority and have the vote."

It actually may come sooner than that.

On April 19, 2018, BBC's Gareth Gordon predicted Catholics might have the majority soon in Northern Ireland. Citing the 2011 census, the Protestant population was at 48%, Catholics 45%. More recently, figures show that of those of working age, 44% are now Catholic and 40% Protestant.[49.]

On April 8, 2021, CNN reported on the continued tensions in parts of Northern Ireland building up around Brexit – the withdrawal of the United Kingdom (UK) from the European Union (EU), which may result in a border between the British-ruled north and the Republic of Ireland in the south, which remains in the European Union.

A border between British controlled Northern Ireland and the Republic of Ireland violates the 1999 peace accord that brought an end to the Troubles.

"Northern Ireland has seen six straight days of violence as unionists and nationalists clashed with police and each other. Brexit-related tensions have been simmering for months, and last week, a decision by police not to prosecute leaders of the Irish nationalist party Sinn Féin for allegedly breaking coronavirus restrictions brought the whole thing to a boil. Now, rioters have clashed along the so-called 'peace line' dividing predominantly unionist and nationalist communities. They've thrown petrol bombs and set a bus on fire. That has been seen as a major breach of trust with Northern Ireland, since the lack of a border had been a key element of the post-1998 peace that followed three decades of violence," the news agency stated.

On June 30, 2021, Susan McKay, writing an op ed piece for the New York Times *Northern Ireland Is Coming to an End*, adds to the perception, that a united Ireland will come to be sooner than later.[50].

"Sinn Féin, (the pro-united Ireland party) is surging ahead in polls in the Irish Republic and may enter government after the next elections in 2025. While around 50 percent of Northern Irish voters back remaining in the United Kingdom, support for Irish unity is growing. Though by no means imminent, that goal has never seemed closer," McKay surmised.

1916 - 2016

In March of 2016, I traveled to Ireland to witness the 100th anniversary of the 1916 Rebellion. The event honored the hundreds of rebels who took over city buildings, including the post office, during the six-day rising proclaiming Irish independence. Before the centenary event in Dublin on Monday, the 28th, I took Bus Eireann to Belfast to attend the unveiling of a statue of James Connolly, the renowned labor and freedom fighter. The statue was designed by artist Steve Feeny.

Dedication of James Connolly statue in Belfast, 2016

By the time I got to Falls Community Council Building on Falls Road in West Belfast, more than a hundred people had gathered around the draped statue. Connolly's great-grandson, James Connolly Heron was speaking.

"This is the best place for James Connolly, in the place where he lived among the people whom he fought for," Heron shouted to the crowd.

Connolly was born in Edinburgh, Scotland to Irish parents. He founded the Irish Citizen Army, an armed and well-trained body of labor men whose aim was to defend workers and strikers from the brutality of the Dublin Metropolitan Police. Opposing British rule overall he fought beside Padraig Pearse and other leaders of the rebellion to establish Irish independence.

Terry O'Sullivan, president of the Laborers' International Union of North America, took the mic next.

"I'm a proud Irish-American whose family comes from County Kerry. I could not be prouder to be an Irishman today. We wouldn't have an Irish American labor movement in the United States of America if it wasn't for 1913 and 1916, because it was the leaders like big Jim Larkin and James Connolly who went to the U.S. and helped form and lead the movement.

"The cause of Ireland is the cause of labor; the cause of labor is the cause of Ireland. This man stood for all the things that makes a decent and just society, like economic and social justice and united and free Ireland. Let's raise our voices in solidarity to make sure his vision, his words, his courage and what he stood for become a reality, that we will become a united Ireland. We will become one country, one government, by the people, of the people and for the people of this great country of Ireland!" he exclaimed passionately.

Terry O'Sullivan, president of the Laborers' International Union of North America, speaking at the James Connolly statue dedication

Back in Dublin, tens of thousands of people from all over the world swelled the city for the 100th anniversary of the 1916 Rebellion, many the Irish diaspora and descendants of the rebels. From my hotel near the Connolly train station, named after James Connolly, I walked down to O'Connell Street, past the post office — one of the many buildings the rebels took claim to 100 years earlier — then over the River Liffey bridge where the historic event was taking place. I was herded along with throngs of people around me. Only people with tickets could get into the inner circle past the ropes; but video monitors had been set up for those who didn't have tickets. It rained lightly as the events took place.

Holding the tricolor, one of tens of thousands of participants at 100th anniversary of the 1916 Rebellion in Dublin

The commemoration began with His Excellency Michael D. Higgins, second-term president of Ireland, laying a wreath at Kilmainham Gaol where 14 of the 16 rebel leaders were executed by the British. Higgins laid another wreath at the General Post Office, the rebel headquarters during the rebellion, before leading a minute's silence for all those who died.

As part of the ceremony, Captain Peter Kelleher from the 27th Infantry Battalion read the Proclamation of Irish independence; members of the Irish army, the police and emergency services paraded through the city, and the Irish Air Corps performed a dramatic fly-by over the General Post office.

Chapter 16 -
Changing Times

When my dad was growing up in Ireland, most of the Irish language had been lost, the British government and its police forces controlled the land, and the Crown's Anglican churches loomed over the citizenry reminding the Irish of England's occupation.

Today, while there's still tension between Catholics and Protestants in the north, there's been a marked reversal of the old order throughout Ireland.

I think my dad would be amazed at the changes.

On a tour of Castlerea's once Anglican church, now renovated and turned into the Trinity Arts Center [51.], I followed Breege Callaghan, the chair of the local arts committee, up to the top floor.

Pointing out a long, rectangular window with a birds-eye view of the town below, she said, "Here, the Anglican bishop would have kept an eye on what was going on in town."

"These are very important times in history. We need to acknowledge that now and write a line in the sand on what happened," said Breege, noting the best way to do that is through the performing arts. The Trinity Arts Centre features Irish plays, poetry forums and dance performances in coordination with the citizenry.

The Trinity Arts Centre, an Irish performing arts centre, was once an Anglican church

"The whole spirit of the building is about community. It is about carrying on our culture, music, dance and drama and embracing the new cultures that have come into our communities," she stressed.

Among featured performances by acknowledged Irish dramatists: *An Ordinary Man* by John McDwyer, *Nobody's Talking to Me* by Tommy Marren, *The Communication Cord* by Brian Friel, and *The Six Marys* by Jean Farrell.

'The Language of the Soul'

Wherever I went in Ireland, signage was in Irish and English, some radio and television shows broadcast in Irish only, and schools, like Oideas Gael of County Donegal, offer Irish language classes for everyone from the very beginner to the knowledgeable speaker.

In 2017, I traveled from Dublin to *Oideas Gael*[52.] to take an Irish language weekend course. It took about seven hours on three buses to get to the school on the other side of the country. There were a lot of stops. In a car it takes around three hours.

Once arrived, it was like reaching the end of the world with the dramatic Atlantic Ocean crashing up against the rocks, changing colors of mountains, lakes, cliffs and winding roads that oversee lush, green pastures and distant dwellings with puffs of spiraling smoke from chimneys. The area is bounded on the south by the mountains of Slieve League (Sliabh Liag) and Leahan and on the north by Slieve Tooey.

The bus driver dropped me off at a bed-and-breakfast and told me to walk up to the school in 30 minutes after I'd gotten settled. I asked him which way that might be since it was dark by that time and I'd lost all sense of direction.

"Up the road there, lass, and take a left," and he was gone.

Making my way in the darkness with the help of my cell phone light, I found the school and inside a flurry of activity as students checked in and were ushered to a classroom, not a word of English spoken. I was of course in the beginner, international student class, never having spoken a word of Irish before in my life.

The classes covered all the basics: greetings — maidin mhaith (good morning), oiche mhaith (good night); ordering food and beverages — pionta (a pint); beoir (beer); bricfeasta (breakfast); lon (lunch); dinnear (dinner); and well wishes — adhmor (good luck); maith thu (well done) to name some.

"Listen," the instructor said, "and repeat what you heard." I went away with a basic understanding of the Irish language and a desire to learn more.

*Mary Whitehair gives students an example of how to start
a story about their families in the Navajo language**

In 2017, writing for the *Navajo Times* [53.] I told the story about Irish and Navajo language loss and revitalization.

"The Navajo language was beaten out of us (in boarding schools)." (Much like the English did to the Irish), said Mary Whitehair who teaches at the To'hajiilee Community School, a Navajo community about 24 miles west from Albuquerque, New Mexico.

"It's sad. You want to communicate with your grandparents," expressed high school senior Tessa Jake, one of Whitehair's students, who hadn't been brought up learning Navajo at home.

Kendra Apachito, also a student in Whitehair's class, felt the same way.

"I want to know about the elders' stories and what life was like when they were growing up," she said.

Across the Atlantic, Geraldine from County Lietrum, who participated in the *Oideas Gael* weekend program, said her original language was the very essence of who she was.

"I think most Irish people have Irish latent in them, and we love it. I think it is good we speak English but we have to get our own language back because for me personally I don't think I express myself in English the same way. The language of my soul is Irish."

"Traditional teachings embedded in the Irish language are lost in English translations. It's very difficult to translate the Irish language into English. It seems that there are no words to express the same sentiment; the essence, the fullness is not there," she added.

For example, in English, the everyday greeting is a simple "Hello."

But, in Irish one might say, "Féadfaidh an bóthar ardú suas chun beannú duit," which translates into English, "May the road rise with you."

"The person is actually wishing you good fortune," explained Geraldine.

Mary Whitehair said it's the same for the Navajo language.

"The core Navajo values are in the language," she stressed.

An Irish language class at Oideas Gael

Curator Kevin O'Shannon talks to visitors at the Culturlann McAdam O'Fiaich in Belfast

The Trinity Arts Center and Oidaes Gael are two examples of how Ireland has reclaimed and rejuvenated Irish culture and history.

Culturlann McAdam O'Fiaich in Belfast is doing the same thing.[54]

Located on Falls Road in Belfast, the Culturlann also operates out of a renovated Anglican church.

The Culturlann includes a bookshop, a café, an art gallery and classrooms.

Stopping in one day, I heard from the corners of the room people chatting in Irish as they drank coffee and ordered traditional foods.

On the day of my visit, the artwork of Gerard Dillon, a well-known Irish painter, was on display. In the bookstore, books by Irish authors and several on Irish language learning sat on shelves. Kevin O'Shannon, a center manager, said that the Culturlann focuses on the arts to support Irish language revitalization.

"Our mission is to promote the Irish language through the arts. It's only through the arts the language has been kept alive," said O'Shannon.

"It provides a sense of identity," he said, adding the Irish language has to be regularly spoken. To encourage the speaking of Irish, "There's an expression in Irish that has become a mantra for Irish speakers here in Belfast. That expression is ná hamháin labhairt faoi, é a dhéanamh which means, 'Don't just talk about it, do it.' You need to be proactive."

He added, "We have a drama society. We put on productions in Irish. We have Irish dancing classes and an Irish language choir."

But he said what patrons like to do the most is drop by, have coffee in the café and speak Irish.

"That's what we need here," said Navajo language teacher Mary Whitehair, referring to the development of Navajo speaking coffee houses, sort of on-the-spot language nests that would give learners places to speak Navajo in English-language dominated areas.

"If that awareness and visibility is there, maybe there will be more participation in speaking (our traditional language)," said Whitehair.

"We need to do this for our youth. We need to put Navajo words back in their mouths so that it's easier for them to start speaking it," she said.

"I want to be able to visit the elders in our community and speak to them," remarked Apachito.

Back at the Culturlann, O'Shannon pointed to the next room. "Take a look in there," he advised, referring to Gerard Dillon's exhibit. Dillon's work gives a personal look at Belfast Street scenes and the surrounding country roads and seaside landscapes documenting everyday activities during the 1970's.

While taking in the intensity of Dillon's work, 1916-1971, I met Peter Joseph Monahan, a gentleman in his 70s, a fluent Irish speaker.

"I think in Irish. It is the proper language of the country. I love Gaelic. It will fade away if it's not spoken every day," he said

"You are a national treasure," I told him.

Peter Joseph Monahan visits Culturlann McAdam O'Fiaich regularly

"I am a rare man," he agreed with a smile and nod of his head.

After my chat with Peter, I walked up to the next level to see an exhibit from New Guinea. There, I met Seamus from Donegal's Innishowen.

"Everything is embedded in the language: culture, history, understanding of the place, values, everything. People like me are really floating on the edge of this culture. We define ourselves when we go abroad. We are Irish and very proud of it," he said.

Then he added, "There's (something wrong with this) idea of historically blaming the English with the demise of Irish language." He noted that, for sure, the Brits caused the loss of the language, but "It's now 100 years since 1916 and what has happened? You can't blame the English for that."

Later, while I was having coffee in the center's café, a group of tourists led by tour guide Bill Rolston came in and sat at the table next to me. After they had settled, I asked Bill why he brought tourists to the Culturlann of all the many places in Belfast.

"I love the place. I love the people you meet in the place. You meet all sorts of people. I never met someone from the *Navajo Times* before, so where else would that happen?"

Rolston's group was from Colombia in South America.

"They're here with their President," he said referring to Juan Manuel Santos.

He explained that the Colombian entourage wanted to visit Belfast because the Irish peace process has been very influential on the Colombian peace process.

"They watch it very carefully, as a model of what to do and not want to do," he mentioned.

He added that the Culturlann is special because it's a living model of language revitalization.

"You will find people sitting next to you speaking Irish. One of the grand old leaders of the Irish language revival was sitting here and you will come here and find teenage kids speaking in Irish. That's wonderful to see," Rolston continued.

O'Shannon said the language would be more supported if the Irish Language Act would ever get passed.

"Unfortunately, the British government has reneged and hasn't put into place various pieces of legislation that would bring an Irish Language Act into full operational existence."

An Irish Language Act would enable people to conduct all of their business in Irish, if they wanted to. For example, the language would be available to be used in the courts and legal documents, he continued.

Native American communities have also begun to decolonize.

As tribal youth rise up, using their voices loud and strong over social and mainstream media, they have demanded the eradication of honoring colonial figures like Christopher Columbus. Today, many cities and states have renamed Columbus Day, Indigenous Peoples' Day.

With pressure from tribal governments, the Native American Languages Act passed in 1990 providing federal grants for teaching, books, materials and productions.

At Ft. Sumner where Navajo people were imprisoned for four years, now there's a Museum commemorating the Long Walk.

Decolonization continues daily as tribes recover lost land and water rights.

My dad would said, "You can't keep a good man (woman) down."

They will rise up to reclaim their own, as they have done on both sides of the Atlantic.

Chapter 17 –
Full circle

My last stay in Castlerea lasted about six months during the winter of 2019 and into 2020. I first stayed at Rita Morgan's Armcashel bed and breakfast because it was like a home away from home by this time.

If you want a real Irish experience, Rita's gracious hospitality is the essence of it all from serving an Irish breakfast to afternoon tea and cookies in the warmth of her multi-story home located on the edge of town overlooking green pastures and fields of very contented cows.

My dear friend Rita Morgan, Armcashel, Castlerea

For my longer stay that year, I rented a bungalow a couple of blocks from Main Street. From where I was staying, Bookalagh was about eight miles away.

By that time, I'd been to Ireland through all four seasons. Don't let anyone fool you, it is cold in Ireland in the winter months, nothing mild about it.

Castlerea holds the history of the O'Conors, the Irish royalty who lost their dynasty to British invasion. The market town also goes down in the history of Ireland since it was here the last shots rang out before a truce was called between Britain and Ireland during the war of independence.

As historians tell it, on July 11, 1921, Sergeant James King of the Royal Irish Constabulary was riding his bicycle on St. Patrick Street, the street where the town's Catholic Church by the same name is located, and was shot dead by two suspected members of the IRA.

Besides this historical event, around Castlerea there are an abundance of historical sites — Ireland's oldest inhabited castle in Donamon; an 11th-Century Celtic cross in Emlagh; St. Brigid's Well in Ballintober; the La Tene stone – 300 B.C – in Castlestrange; remnants of ancient oak wood in Ballygar; a ringfort and prehistoric burial mounds in Rahtra; and St. Patrick's Holy Well in Kilmore, to mention some.

For nature lovers, Castlerea's Suck Valley Way takes you off the beaten path past peat bogs to wildflower meadows, native woodlands, disappearing lakes called turloughs and overgrown marshes. Here you can enjoy the heart of Ireland walking, angling or cycling by day and at night enjoy local company, spirits and food at Hester's or Tully's on Main street. For breakfast and lunch, stop into Benny's for fresh meats and homegrown vegetables and scrumptious baked goods.

Acts of kindness are part of the everyday interactions. It's the fabric that runs throughout the country.

Each day, I was the recipient of more than one. It would begin in the morning at Armcashel with Rita Morgan greeting me with a bright

"Good morning!" along with breakfast however I wanted it and tea or coffee. During the day, a newly acquainted friend would meet me for tea in the afternoon, give me a ride, show me exactly where to go when lost, and often it would be prefaced with "Are you OK, now?" When I told them why I was in town, they would say, "Good woman, you are brilliant."

One day walking down a street in Roscommon Town, I asked the young woman walking hurriedly towards me if I was going the right way to the library. She said 'Yes,' turned to go on her way, then thinking twice about it, turned back and said she would give me a ride there, no problem.

And every week during our wellness class in Roscommon Town, Elizabeth took me to lunch most often at the historic Abbey Hotel where we would have long, interesting chats, and then dropped me off wherever I needed to go next, which was usually the library.

One day I took a taxi to Ballaghaderreen to attend a conference on Douglas Hyde, the first president of Ireland. There, I met Mary and Ethel, both with the Roscommon Heritage Society. After the conference, Mary offered to take me to a few sites: the bog, a deserted convent by the lake that looks like a scene out of Camelot, and the 19th-Century church at Fairymount where she was baptized and married.

On any given day, while traveling around, I would see familiar faces, like Jerry from the Roscommon Town community radio station, or run into Mary in Roscommon Town. But, most often, I met townspeople at the bus stop. One day, I met Asia who is originally from an island near Madagascar. She's married to an Irishman from Roscommon. She had a charming personality and a joyous nature. It was so nice to chat and we agreed it was nice here in Ireland where people always stop to talk to you and say "Hello." Then, the bus came and she went off to Longford and I waited for the bus to Castlerea.

While in Castlerea that winter, I visited Finbar McNamara and my cousin Noel in Ballymoe, experienced an Irish Christmas with Rita and her family in Galway, joined a "greener-you" class and learned how each person can make a difference in the world's carbon overload, took a tour with the Williamstown Historic society to Arigna, an historic coal mining town and befriended Jean Higgins, took a health class in Roscommon Town, and spent hours in the library there, often stopping into the local pub or the popular Gleeson's restaurant before catching the last bus back to Castlerea.

One day, I had the good fortune to meet Jacinta, while waiting in line at Castlerea's Bank of Ireland. A few months later, masks and six-feet distances mandated, this serendipitous meeting may not have happened.

That's when I told her that I was writing a story about my dad's early life in Ireland and the historical events he witnessed, like the 1916 rebellion and the subsequent civil war, which he most likely participated in. From that day until today, she's been a driving force behind the book's production – arranging the talk at the Tarmon National school, introducing me to Jimmy Ganly, her uncle-in-law Padraig Beatty and her brother Gary who in turn introduced me to Michael Hanly.

"Come on, I want to show you something," Jacinta said one day.

We drove a little way out of the town's centre to a memorial to Paddy Flynn, Paddy Conry and James Monds, soldiers "who gave their lives for the cause of Irish independence 1920-1921."

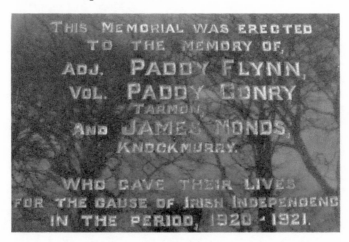

This memorial is dedicated to Irish soldiers fighting for a united Ireland during the civil war

At the entrance of the Tarmon National School, students pass by the memorial every day, Jacinta pointed out.

Built in 1890, the Tarmon National School is one of 15 change-maker schools in Ireland. Changemaker schools utilize a wide variety of innovative approaches which value inclusion, human rights, empathy, creativity and teamwork to name some. In 1916, principal of the school was Daniel O'Rourke.

"It would be shocking that you would be passing Tarmon National School, writing a book about what is right outside their door, and they (wouldn't know about it). It's such a unique opportunity and it should be shared with the children," she said.

On Dec. 5th, 2019, she worked with educators Kieran Dodd, Marie Baggott and Gregory Kelly to arrange for the school presentation, so the children could learn about my undertaking and the steps my father took throughout the 20th Century.

One student, Dylan Keane, asked if we could be related. And another student, Sean Silk, expressed interest in the school my dad went to and hoped that one day it would be preserved for its history. Others commented on what it must have been like to emigrate at the time, dealing with quarantine, disease, and the obstacles to getting to America and then finding work.

They were well versed in Irish history.

"(Learning about Colleen's dad) made the history more personal and they could relate. I'm pretty sure Colleen (enhanced) their awareness of what the people before them have done," Jacinta commented.

Students Michele Henry (holding the Advent calendar) and Ava Croghan from the Tarmon National School, Jacinta Greene-Beatty (right), and myself (middle) take a moment for a photo after my presentation on my dad's life story.

During my stay in Castlerea that winter before the corona virus pandemic, Rita Morgan and I searched for my grandmother's and uncles' gravesites. According to her death certificate, my grandmother Bridget died "of senility" at 81 on January 18, 1951. Her daughter, Delia, my aunt, registered her death a couple of months later. A couple of years later, my Uncle James passed away.

I was told they would have been buried in the old section of the Kilcroan cemetery most likely with my grandpa, Bernard Sr.

My grandmother was laid to rest in Kilcroan graveyard

Stopping at one of the ancient Celtic crosses and hefty stone monuments in the graveyard, we worked at dusting off the white lichen that made it hard to read the inscriptions. Historian Jimmy Ganly advised the best way to read the inscriptions without doing any harm is to get red or green pavement chalk and rub it flat across the surface of the stone and all the white will turn the color that you are using.

And, if the headstone is lying flat on the ground, sprinkle talcum powder on it. Then, using a paint brush, spread the talcum powder in one direction and the powder will fill in the letters.

He said, looking dismayed, that some people use bleach, which is very damaging. "Some of those inscriptions have been there for 200 to 300 years." He also warned not to use grass. "Grass is very acidic," he said.

But, even after uncovering the inscriptions without causing any damage, there were no signs of my grandpa, grandma or uncles Patrick and James or the child Bridget in the old Kilcroan cemetery.

We did find my Uncle Michael's and Aunt Mary's distinctive memorials in the new cemetery. Paying our respects, we said a prayer for them as the rain gently fell in a veiled mist.

Rita suggested continuing our search in the Moore Cemetery down the road.

"They could be there," she said.

Grass and mud had built up at the bottom of the gate of the cemetery making it impossible to open the gate. So, we climbed up the gate and jumped over.

We didn't find my grandparents or uncles or Bridget there either, but we did find an ancient Celtic cross marker for James Keane. The time period was right, around the end of the 19th century, but uncertainty crept in when Mary was identified on the stone as James' wife, and not Margaret.

Moore Cemetery marker for a 19th Century James Keane

KEANE is etched into the bottom of the ancient Celtic cross

Thinking about possibilities, Rita said, "It could be that her full name was Mary Margaret. They did that a lot back then."

Jimmy Ganly said no matter what they were most likely together because families often buried their kin in the same plot.

"You will invariably find that the graveyard is higher up. Some are five or six feet higher than the surrounding fields because there are so many bodies in there."

Even though I didn't find my kin, I felt a closeness to them. They were there somewhere and I sensed they knew they were being remembered.

Isn't that what we all want, after we die?

Chapter 18 -
Crashing an American Wake

Over 150 years, despite the Big Wind, the Great Famine, poverty, evictions, wars, and emigration, the Keane family held onto the cottage and significantly increased their land holdings.

Helen Gavin McHugh painted this picture of the cottage and gave it to my brother Brian

On a land valuation record dated 1911, Bernard Sr., my grandfather, held 20 acres, 1 rood, 1 perch, paying 6 pounds and 1 shilling a year for the annual payment. It was a significant increase from the approximately 1 ½ acres my great-grandfather James farmed.

On another valuation record dated 1932, Bernard Sr.'s name is crossed off and Bridget's (my grandmother) name is written above it; land holdings 28 acres, 1 rood; payment 6 pounds, 11 shillings. Since my grandfather had passed away four years earlier in 1928, there must have been an ongoing discussion on how and when my grandmother was going to travel to the land office in Dublin to update the record.

When my grandmother passed away in 1951, the land transferred to my Uncle John who farmed the land his entire life. He passed away on August 10, 1996 at 85 years of age. The land is still in the Keane family.

Uncle John, dad's youngest brother

During my dad's lifetime, although he didn't say much about all he had done and witnessed since leaving his mom and the cottage as a young man, his life spanning most of the 20th century speaks for itself: the witnessing and participation in historical events in Ireland, the uncertain passage to a future life in America, surviving the Great Depression and receiving a Purple Heart for combat injuries during WWII. As a provider to his family, he contributed to the automobile and aeronautics industry before, during and after the war.

On one of my last drives with Rita Morgan, we drove once again past the land where my grandmother's cottage once stood.

Here, I'm standing at the location of where my grandma's cottage stood

Remains of what might be the Keane cottage's back wall seen through the foliage

"See," Rita said, "you can still see the remnants of the house. That was probably the back wall," she surmised, pointing to a crumbling section of rocks covered with foliage.

I wondered about the generations of Keanes who lived in the cottage through the famine, the rebellion, the civil war and war of independence and then the transition to Irish independence.

I imagined the happy times that took place, the meals and chats and storytelling around the fire, a dance or two in the front room.

But that last visit is not my last memory of the cottage, nor had I forgotten the promise I made to go back to Ireland with my dad.

On the night of the voice mail message from my mom when my dad came to visit me on his way to the other world, he hadn't left quite yet after all. Without me noticing, he had moved from the chair on the other side of the room and there he was sitting next to me on the couch. I took his hand and closed my eyes.

He closed his.

And I made the wish.

In an instant, still holding hands, we were at my grandma's cottage in Bookalagh. Smoke was billowing out of the chimney; Rebel, Brian's black and white border collie was hanging around the front door. Several people were gathered inside and others were walking up the road to the cottage.

I let go of his hand as he walked in. As he passed through the door, he was young again and dressed in American street clothes from the 1930s, as dashing as Cilian Murphy in Peaky Blinders.

As the people began to recognize him, a roar went up.

"It's Brian! He's come home." As he stepped inside his brothers and sisters greeted him with hugs and kisses and his mom came out from the kitchen and wrapped her arms around him.

"I thought I would never see you again. And here you are on the anniversary of your American Wake. We have it every year," she said, letting tears flow freely this time.

"I promised I'd come back, Mammy," he said, handing her a bouquet of flowers he had picked along the way.

Tearing up, she took his hand and guided him to the best chair near the fire.

"Now Brian, tell us what you've been up to and we'll tell you the same."

He looked back at me and gave me his familiar wink. I smiled back at him. He was home again and finally at peace.

The next morning, I awoke with a new sense of identity.

I am a Keane, O'Cathain, Cailin Ni' Chathain in Irish, and on my grandmother's side of the family, a descendent of the O'Connor dynasty.

And my dad, Brian Keane from Bookalagh, was a hero.

My Dad

Barney and Jovita Keane's Legacy

My dad and mom's legacy is carried on by my brothers and me, seven grandchildren: my daughter Joanna; Patrick, Danny, Dennis and Kate (Jerry and Peg's children); Michael and Chris (Mary and Brian's children); and seven great-grandchildren: D.J., Gracie and Sarah (Chris and Jennifer's children), Kiera and Cooper (Katie and Chad's children), and Rylan and Aubrey (Dennis and Katy's children).

As a civil engineer, my brother Brian went on to build a successful engineering company, TMI, based in Florida; Jerry worked as a high-level manager for major U.S. companies and with his wife Peg owned and operated Keane's Religious Goods in Mission Viejo, California; and I followed my passion as a journalist to report on social justice issues in documentary and print formats, mostly for the Navajo Times in recent years.

My daughter, Joanna Keane Lopez, has earned recognition in the field of art for designing and preserving traditional structures made out of earthen materials, carrying on her Spanish and Irish heritages; my nephew, Patrick Keane expresses his creativity and humor at systems and structures of all kinds as a standup comic; my nephew Dennis, an all-star basketball player in high school and college, followed in his father's footsteps as a businessman, and Katie is an accomplished athletic trainer. Danny, Jerry and Peg's oldest son, has shown us all how to endure beyond the hardship of physical challenges in good cheer and with a loving heart.

Describing grandson Christopher, Brian and Mary's oldest son, my brother Jerry once remarked on his open heart, kindness and good cheer. Christopher and his wife Jennifer reach out and help where-ever needed. Jerry added, "That's what makes them great!" Grandson Michael, an audio engineer, has carried on his grandpa's workmanship, independence and fortitude owning and operating his own engineering business like his dad.

My daughter Joanna and me

Granddaughter Joanna Keane Lopez

Brian Keane (back row, left), Michael, Donna, DJ, Katy, Dennis, Christopher, Jennifer
Mary Keane (front row, left) Gracie, Sarah (Chris and Jennifer's children),
Ryan and Aubrey, (Dennis and Katy's children)

Grandson Christopher Keane and his wife, Jennifer

Grandson Michael Keane and his wife, Donna

Grandson Danny Keane

Danny and his grandma

Great grandchildren, Kiera, Cooper, Rylan and Aubrey
and their grandma Peg (Margaret), Jerry's wife

Granddaughter Katie, her husband Chad and great grandchildren Kiera and Cooper

Finbar McNamara and Katie Keane Jackson at the 2003 Keane Reunion

Grandson Patrick has the flair for the stage, like his great uncle James

Grandson Dennis makes an outstanding play for his Santa Margarita high school team

My brother Jerry and my mom, Jovita Keane

Sadly, my mom and my brother Jerry are no longer with us. My mom passed away when she was 91. Jerry died way too young. He was 59.

Jerry and his wife Peg

Brian and his wife Mary

The Author's Parting Words

Go n-ardóidh an bóthar suas chun bualadh leat!

May the road rise up to greet you!

REFERENCES

1. Clifdenheritage.org/a-picture-of-the-famine-in-Connemara/

2. Yourirish.com/history/17th-century/flight-of-the-earls\

3. Wikipedia – Irish protest, English retaliation

4. Indigenous Voices of the Colorado Plateau, Northern Arizona University

5. Bosqqueredondomemorial.com

6. Kinghouse.ie

7. Navajonationmuseum.org

8. National Hispanic Cultural Center, Nhccnm.org

9. Ibw21.org/
   editors-choice/a-brief-history-of-us-concentration-camps/

10. Castlerea.ie/the-history-of-castlerea/

11. The Impact of the Wyndham Land Act 1903 on County Galway by Tom Tonge.

12. Irish land divisions - and how these impact on genealogy records - irish-genealogy-toolkit.com

13. Background to Landed Estates - askaboutireland.ie)

14. Ballymoe, John J. Brady, published by St. Croan's Church Parish Council, Ballymoe, County Galway, Ireland, Sept. 2005.

15. AskaboutIreland.ie - The Irish Language in the 19th Century

16. County Roscommon Historical and Archaeological Society Journal, Vol 13

17. Four Mile House Ambush by Gillian Greene

18. Wikipedia, War of Independence, Bloody Sunday

19. Ireland-calling.com – Irish war of independence – essential facts

20. Clonalishouse.com

21. Irelandxo.com/ireland-xo/visiting/
    clonalis-house-seat-oconnor-don

22. Family Heritage Centre, Dublin, Ireland

23. Idaho & Pacific Northwest History Collection

24. Warhistoryonline.com

25. Facinghistory.org

26. History.com/topics/world-war-ii/the-holocaust

27. Historicdetroit.org/buildings/continental-motors

28. Michiganhistory.leadr.msu.edu/

29. Wikipedia.org – military use of children

30. Militaryyearbookproject.com/references/general-references/
    army-replacement- trainingcenters

31. Operation Nordwind 1945, Hitler's last offensive in the West by
    Steven Zaloga, Osprey Printing, 2010

32. Warfarehistory.com – Nordwind the other battle of the Bulge,
    Flint Whitlock

33. Eisenhower's Thorn on the Rhine – The Battles for the Colmar
    Pocket, 1944-45 by Nathan Prefer, Casemate Publishers, 2015

34. The Forty-Fifth Infantry Division, The Combat Report of an
    Infantry Division

35. 45thdivision.org/Campaigns Battles/Reipertswiller.htm

36. WWII U.S. Medical Research Centre 11th field hospital unit history

37. Med-dept.com/unit-histories/11th-field-hospital/

38. Warfarehistorynetwork.com/2018/12/22/ nordwind-the-other-battle-of-the-bulge/

39. Lone Sentry —Service: Story of the Signal Corps," published by the Stars & Stripes in Paris in 1944-1945.

40. Wikipedia, The Signal Corps

41. Historicdetroit.org/buildings/continental-motors

42. After the Guns Have Been Laid Down published in 2014 and Where the Rubber Misses the Road in 2015, colleenankeane@ gmail.com

43. Independent.co.uk, Irishidentity.com, history.com

44. Northern Ireland Community Relations Council, community-re-lations.org.uk

45. YouTube video: the Ardoyne protest

46. Rioting breaks out in Ardoyne, Belfast 2015 - YouTube

47. How the Troubles Began: a timeline, the Irishtimes.com

48. Wikipedia – Falls Road Belfast

49. BBC News, Easter Rising Commemoration

50. nytimes.com/2021/06/30/opinion/northern-ireland-centenary.html

51. Trinity Arts Center, castlerearts.com

52. Oideas Gael, oideas-gael.com

53. Navajo Times, navajotimes.com

54. Culturlann McAdam O Fiaich, culturlann.ie

Especially Important Contacts

- Armcashel Bed and Breakfast, Castlerea, County Roscommon, Rita Morgan owner, ritamorgan@armcashel.com, website: armcashel.com

- Castlerea Library, Knock Road Castlerea, Co. Roscommon, F45 C8P7, Branch Librarian: Breege Beirne, Tel. 094 9620745 Email: castlerealibrary@roscommoncoco.ie

- The Lore of Ireland, An Encyclopedia of Myth, Legend and Romance by Daithí Ó hÓgáin

- Ellis Island heritage - Heritage.statueofliberty.org

- Tarmon National School, tarmonns.ie. office@tarmonns.ie

- Certificates of birth, death, marriage - Government Offices, Convent Road, County Roscommon, F42 VX53, gro@welfare.ie +353 90 6632900

- Land records - Land Registry Office, Suite 10267, 77 Sir John Rogerson's Quay, Dublin 2 Eircode D02F54 www.landregistryireland.com

- County Roscommon, Ireland F42 VR98 Tel: 090 6637100 Email: info@roscommoncoco.ie, www.gov.ie

- Williamston Heritage Society – heritage.galwaycommunityheritage.org

- National Personnel Records Center (NPRC)

- 1 Archives Drive

- St. Louis, Missouri 63138

- 314-801-0800

- www.archives.gov

- bbc.co.uk/history/historic_figures/de_valera_eamon.shtml